THE FIVE AGES OF THE CINEMA

THE
FIVE AGES
OF THE
CINEMA

CHARLES H. TARBOX

AN EXPOSITION-BANNER BOOK

Exposition Press   *Smithtown, New York*

First Edition

© 1980 by Charles H. Tarbox

Library of Congress Catalog Card Number: 80-66983

ISBN 0-682-49618-9

Printed in the United States of America

THE FIVE AGES OF THE CINEMA

Introduction

Motion pictures are now (1980) eighty-five years old. They started in 1895. It is my hope that I will impart to my readers an understanding of the way the cinema has changed over these years. It has had distinct periods. That which seems lasting and eternal is not lasting, and it is replaced. Each period of the art begins, flourishes, then dies. Some of the forms are quiescent for many years only to bloom again suddenly.

The period of the individual creator ended for all practical purposes in the early feature era. Yet after many years it blazed again in the cinematheque and the experimental films of the late 1960s. There is a close kinship between the French "magic" films of Melies and the Pathé Frères and recent individualistic films produced in exactly the same way with most modest cost sheets and highly interesting imaginations.

The wild Sennett slapsticks were to end with the silent era, but their technique appears again and again in later films, most recently in *Mad, Mad, Mad, Mad World.*

There are at least five separate periods of moviemaking. The first lasted from 1895 to 1903; it was an experimental period. All that existed were short films, without plot, that relied entirely upon scenes of motion to interest and to hold an audience. The second period began with the filming of *The Great Train Robbery* in 1903 and continued for not less than eight years, until 1911. This was the era of the story film but a story film held to an arbitrary time limit of one reel. It took all of these years, at least sixteen, for the foreign filmmakers to produce *Homer's Odyssey* and, in America, for Selig to make *The Two Orphans* and for Griffith to make *Enoch Arden.* Three more years were to pass before *The Birth of a Nation* was to be filmed. This third period, the era of the silent feature film, was to last until it was replaced by the era of the talkies in 1927. The fifth period began with the advent of television and its

1

effect upon the movie-going public. The effect of television is generally credited with responsibility for the decline in mass movie attendance and in the changes recently seen in the medium. This is not necessarily so. Other factors contributed to its decline, as well. In this book, however, greatest detail will be given to early years, because they are the least known and yet the most fundamental. The period from 1911 to 1916 represents the motion picture in its fantastic growth. It was to rival the printed word as a mass medium. It did not have to meet the challenge of radio or television. As a business, it was to offer opportunities for profits beyond those of any previous period. And it was to offer them to many and varied individuals of most diverse backgrounds.

Many of the excellent books that have been written about the early movie years are reminiscences of individuals who had a part in those years. This one is not. I have read and enjoyed most of them, but I have been disappointed in them because of what they have left out. I have tried in this work to give a cross section of the releases, the business changes, the growth of theaters, and, above all, the vast extent of the early cinema. No one film represents a period. No individual is alone representative. Sources of the statements made in this book are from my collection of trade publications. Reviews in some instances are from these same sources. Direct comments on individual films have been made only when I have seen the film.

This book is part one of a projected two-part work. It is a rapid survey of the industry, with the glib idea that what I remember and think to be important—is. The second part will be a detailed documentation, year by year, with statistics that I hope will support my conclusions.

It must be remembered that there are three distinct divisions of the industry: production, distribution, and exhibition. Production can be understood. Exhibition can be understood. The most complex and least understood is distribution, or the middle ground between the studio and the theater. Distribution is important, perhaps most important, because if it does not function properly, the flow of funds to the studios stops, and the amount and quality of films to be produced is immediately affected. Likewise, if distribution is too effective, serves the studios too well and thereby drains the theaters of money needed for them to function, the eventual result is to choke off the box office income, and it is from this source alone that the money comes with which to produce films.

The interplay of the forces behind studios, distribution, and theaters is in an almost constant state of change. This change is reflected in the type of film produced and shown; without an understanding of the way it operates, it is difficult to understand the cinema. From time to time, films have been made that did not fit into the current format of operation, seen by only a small fraction of the public that might have been interested in them. Some of them were rated as artistic triumphs but commercial failures. From my point of view, a film that does not reach an audience is not important. The ones that are important are the ones that do reach many audiences.

The years from 1911 to 1917 are years in which more films were made each year than in any years before or since. They were years in which individuals were able to enter freely into the production or the distribution or the showing of films with very little money. In each of these years, more films were available to American audiences than in any decade of recent times. More movie theaters were in operation. More people went frequently to the movies. The opportunity to engage in any part of the motion picture business was widely available.

If we say that a later era should be considered the most important era of the films instead of the one described above, we would be right if we are talking of only important, individual pictures. But even in thinking along these lines, we must recognize that the players who appeared in these later films, the men who directed and produced them, the distributors who controlled them, and the theater men who exhibited them almost to a man came into importance from their experiences during the early years. The exceptions are the men of wealth who arrived on the scene later. After 1916, it became necessary to have access to substantial capital funds to make a film or a series of films. It also became necessary to have a record of success to appear in them as a player, to photograph them as a cameraman, or to direct them. This did not block the appearance of new talents from other fields—the stage and, later, radio—but it was no longer simple to get an opportunity to be part of the film. Star names of the 1920s like Mary Pickford, Charlie Chaplin, William S. Hart, Tom Mix, Norma and Constance Talmadge, Lillian and Dorothy Gish, Mae Marsh—all were veterans of the early years. D. W. Griffith, Mack Sennett, Thomas H. Ince, Irving S. Cummings, Frank Borzage, David Butler, Irving Thalberg, Robert Z. Leonard, James Cruze, Henry King, and many many more in production and direction date back to the era about which I write. Even the theaters in which the later films were projected were in many instances controlled by men whose humble beginnings go back to the important early years.

The feature picture was to make the movie big business. It was to create masterpieces of far greater critical acclaim than the ones about which I write. But they were to come from a closely controlled central source, access to which was denied the ordinary man.

There were already in the 1960s indications that a return to the days of the individual filmmaker was on its way. The small cinematheque, the film clubs, the art theater, and the wide and diversified nontheatrical groups all united to offer a place to exhibit a modest film for a modest rental. Television has taken over the mass market. There is now, as never since the earliest years of the cinema, an opportunity for the individual with a small supply of money and an idea.

As we go into the 1980s, it may be that another evolutionary step is at hand. It is too early to determine if cable TV is that "new" step. It is still television in the sense that it is viewed in the privacy of the home—not among a theater audience. However, the fact that it runs without interruptions by commercials means that it does have the cumulative power of the best cinema.

Theta Cable TV in Los Angeles has started to give us short films like *Oh, Brother, My Brother*, a fourteen-minute film that is a special look at two youngsters—five-year-old Josh Lowell and his two-year-old brother, Evan. This is a return to the variety program format of the earliest years of the cinema. It is a marvelous bit of filmmaking: patience, tenderness, and talent—all without the need for large finances. *Oh, Brother, My Brother* is only one of some delightful little films that Theta has begun to offer. There are other programs available on Theta that suggest that cable TV will expand far beyond the limits of either the cinema or commercial television.

But comments like this properly belong in a book to be written at the end of the 1980s, not at its beginning.

Movies were first shown in 1895. It must not be supposed that there was no entertainment industry prior to that time. There was. Every large city in the country had a number of theaters devoted to stage entertainment. In some of these theaters, notably in New York, new plays were produced each year, and the attendance at these stage plays was greater than has ever since been possible. There were, in addition, theaters devoted to vaudeville and to burlesque. Vaudeville consisted of variety entertainment of many different types. A typical bill would include acrobats or tumblers, a magician, a song and dance team, and perhaps one act from a full-length play that had recently closed on the legitimate stage. Stars like the Drews, John Barrymore, and many more were eager and willing to play in vaudeville theaters after their stage shows closed. Burlesque, originally, was just what the name implies, a parody of other shows, of current events, of political affairs, and in many ways it was as much general entertainment as was vaudeville. The greatest difference between the legitimate stage and the vaudeville and burlesque stages was in the cost of the tickets. Necessarily, the stage was the most costly and its productions the most elaborate. One of the talked-of stage shows was *Ben Hur*; the chariot race was presented on the stage in New York with the horses racing on moving rollers. This same effect was later created for the horse race in *In Old Kentucky*.

Elaborate change-of-scene equipment and complex stage settings were needed for such shows as *The Bluebird*; here intricate arrangements of scenery and lights were needed that involved the work of many stagehands and musicians. In musical plays, large orchestras were employed.

The greatest difference between the stage of this period and the cinema that was to follow was that the stage could display the talents of a personality only at one location. This location was, first of all, New York. Stars who made a success in a play on the New York stage were held for a year or more, and people who did not live in New York or who did not come to New York could satisfy their interest in the theater only by reading about the New York theater in a magazine or newspaper.

It was possible, of course, to move the original Broadway company to Chicago or to Buffalo or to Pittsburgh after the New York run had ended. This was done. The stage in 1895 and for many years thereafter was national, meaning that it did extend over the entire country. The "road," as it was called, was the area outside of New York City, and the leading stars did appear in cities other than New York. It was customary to play several engagements prior to the New York opening; the reception in these engagements helped to make the play run smoothly at the time of the New York opening. Changes could be made, the show could be tightened up and improved, and audiences in New Haven, Boston, Philadelphia, and other cities were often given an advance opportunity to see a hit Broadway show.

After the New York run had ended, the show could go on tour. Here the choice was often open to a popular star either to go on tour with the hit of the previous season or to open in a new play on Broadway. Many of the great old troupers did go on tour and names such as Joseph Jefferson, Sarah Bernhardt, John Drew, Richard Mansfield, and many more were known in all the cities from coast to coast. However, because the cost of transportation of a show from one city to another was large, there was a constant tendency to let the economic factors influence the way the show went on. Many times a hit show would go on the road with a cast of actors different, in whole or in part, from the cast of the same show on Broadway. One of the very successful performers for out-of-New York engagements was Harry Lauder, who made many a farewell trip from coast to coast. His style of entertainment was highly personal. He did not need scenic effects or a large cast to be effective. Harry Lauder was as great an attraction in the smallest town in which he appeared as he was in London or Edinburgh or New York.

As I have indicated, the demand for the best plays and the best stars was far beyond the supply. New York had first call. Major cities in the east from Boston to Washington were favored in the try-out engagements prior to the New York opening. Cities such as Pittsburgh, Buffalo, Detroit, Chicago, and Cincinnati could expect a season of stage attractions that would include a few appearances of a hit show from the last New York season and quite a few former New York hits with different stars; in addition, there were always vaudeville and burlesque attractions for these cities. In the Far West and in the Deep South, the going was a little tougher. Shows came but not as often. In the smaller cities—the Madisons, the Grand Rapids, the Elmiras, and the Little Rocks—it was truly a rare event for an original New York show to play at their theaters.

Yet these cities all did have theaters, as did thousands of other towns, down to some very small ones, indeed. One of the first things to be done by the newly rich of Central City in Colorado was to build a theater and to make ready for that great day when Sarah Bernhardt would be available to step on the stage. There was a hunger in all hearts for the theater, and it was a civic enterprise of great importance to satisfy that demand. Guarantees were posted of very substantial sums; ticket selling went on for weeks prior to the opening of an important show; and at Central City and at thousands of other cities of modest size there was a complete sellout for the rare top star who was willing to appear in a one-night stand. Grosses secured from a series of six appearances in six different cities could be greater than the receipts in New York. In a day when the workingman's wages were a dollar a day, theater tickets for top shows cost from three to five dollars and if there was a sellout, scalpers got even more.

Into this situation came a great mass of small-time operators—some much more small-time than the others. Some cities maintained a stock company with a resident cast of players and each week a new play was offered. In Milwaukee, such a company was directed by Edwin Thanhouser of whom we will hear more when we finally do begin to talk about the cinema. A popular form of show for the smaller towns was called the "tab show," or tabloid, a mongrel type of musical comedy. A small cast who could sing and dance and tell jokes made an evening pass very pleasantly. *Uncle Tom's Cabin* was on tour; it is said that during one season fifty-four different companies offered this play in all parts of the country. Some of the productions may have been very bad and great fun has been made of them; however, their appearance was welcomed in towns that were literally starved for entertainment.

We must go down the line to find all the different shows that were traveling about. Actors who could not quite make the grade on Broadway or even in the road shows that played the larger cities went on tour in the smaller cities. Some of them stayed for a week with a repertoire of six different plays; others offered a curious blend of vaudeville and burlesque; still others styled themselves as lecturers and gave appearances that were supposed to be cultural. These last frequently carried with them a stereopticon, or magic lantern, and illustrated their lectures with slides. The slides were usually of places like the Holy Land, the Grand Canyon, and, probably in the western states, New York and the Great White Way. Comic slides would be added "for the children." Perhaps the lecturer or his wife would also sing a song or do a dance or tell a funny story.

It was into this environment that the movie was born in 1895. Its first appearances were in the larger cities and the first of these was as one of the acts on a program that featured vaudeville. The movie developed in many different ways and I do not want to overlook the development of small store-show theaters in the cities, which were entirely an affair of the movie. However, on a country-wide basis, it was as an added attraction or supplement to previous forms of entertainment that the movie made its debut.

I think of the first movies as "slides that moved." They were exactly that. They were a single scene thrown on a screen as a slide had been thrown on a screen, but the motion picture had movement and action. The scene could be of a fire station in which the doors would open and the fire horses and equipment rush out and dash away down the street. The scene could be of a railroad track in which in the distance a train would be seen approaching until it ran directly into the camera. Other scenes might be of bathers on a beach, of war ships, of traffic in a large city. Comics were quickly added, to wit, a small boy who tipped over the fruit vendor's wagon.

One of the first films made in France showed the employees of Louis Lumière leaving the factory where they were employed to make films and projectors. It sold many hundreds of copies. An early Edison masterpiece was called *The Kiss*. This short film was nothing more than an enlarged picture of John Rice kissing May Irwin. It lasted a minute or so. It was what we would later on call a close-up. A movie program of these early days was actually a collection of a dozen or more of these short lengths. It lasted fifteen minutes or so and was supplemented by the lecture, the vaudeville show, or the stage attraction, which it helped to stretch out time-wise.

Rather quickly the novelty of "pictures that move" wore off, and the movies were then relegated to the end of a vaudeville bill in the vaudeville theaters. There they remained for many many years to be known as "the chaser," which was a term that illustrates their greatest value to the management. The sophisticates of that day, having seen one or more movies and having no great desire to see another, would leave during the movie part of the program; their seats could be then sold again to those who were waiting for the next show.

There were, however, other uses to be made of the movie. One of the first was the Hale Tour Cars, which first were used at the St. Louis exhibition and which later were located in the downtown areas of many cities. These theaters, for they were theaters, were fitted to look like a train, with seats like train seats and sometimes with rollers to simulate the motion of a train. Those who purchased tickets could see a motion picture of scenery at the front of the car; the illusion was that you were taking a trip. Far more dignity was given to the Hale Tour Films than to any previous films; there was no attempt to add comics or to make the program anything except a movie of travel films. Many of the railroads financed the films shown in this manner.

Still another use of the movies was in tents, black-top tents that could move from town to town like a carnival or circus but that showed movies. These programs in some respects drew from the carnival background of their managers, and comedians, singers, dancers, and the like may well have accompanied the films. There is the story of one such operation that was elaborate in the extreme. A thin spray of water was projected into the air; colored lights were played upon it; the movie was projected on the film of water—all to the accompaniment of musical instruments and songs. This was called the "Yellow Top." It was reported to be filled to capacity, while competitors with black tops and movies alone were empty. Fairs would often have more than one Black Top on the midway and competition became acute.

To meet this competition, production began of a series of films that were supposed to illustrate events from the Spanish American War. A most intricate film was contrived that showed the battle of Manila Bay. Another film showed nurses on the battlefield. Many of these films came from William N. Selig, of Chicago, who not many years later was to ask permission of Theodore Roosevelt to accompany him on his trip to Africa. Since his letter was not answered, Mr. Selig reproduced the African trip in his studio in Chicago with the help of some animals in the zoo. It is said that Roosevelt was vastly amused and did not interfere. But I am getting ahead of our story.

There were at the turn of the century several manufacturers of motion picture projectors and film. The first, Thomas A. Edison, was then more interested in his other activities than he was in the motion picture. He had plans to synchronize the film with his phonograph and to offer movies that talked. He had other plans as well. He looked for profits from his motion picture department to come from sales of the projectors primarily; he considered the film a necessary evil since projectors could not be sold unless films also were available. The other manufacturer, Biograph, was interested primarily in films for showing in vaudeville houses, and their film was much larger than the Edison film, having dimensions much like those of a later-day Cinerama. Biograph also had interests, as did Edison, in the peep show parlors, where a short film sequence could be seen by putting a penny in a slot. An arcade in Buffalo, in the basement of the Ellicott Square Building, had peep show machines and also a theater of sorts that ran the actual movie films on a small screen and that could accommodate ten or a dozen people at one time. Other early manufacturers were the ingenious Mr. Selig of Chicago, Mr. Sigmund Lubin of Philadelphia, and Smith, Rock, and Blackton of Vitagraph.

Edison had little or no interest in film manufacture at this time, and all work in this department of his enterprises was delegated. Edwin V. Porter, a bright young man, was put in charge, and in 1903 he produced *The Great Train Robbery*, a landmark film. This film ran for almost fifteen minutes at the then standard film speed. It told a story. It had a large cast. A train is held up; the robbers escape and are hunted down. This film literally breathed the breath of life into the movie. A copy was purchased by the Warner brothers and was the start of their career. It is said that a small store-show in Pittsburgh gave continuous exhibitions of *The Great Train*

Robbery, from early morning until late at night. Programs of this era would feature *The Great Train Robbery* with, perhaps, several of the earlier short films. Program length was never more than half an hour and could be shorter if the crowd outside was large. The audience went in the front door and out the side door or the back door. In a theater with a hundred seats or less, it was possible to accommodate several thousand people in a day. The first real theater in Buffalo, the Hippodrome, later to be known as the Little Hippodrome, literally took in bushel baskets full of nickels. In one day, the receipts were over $300, meaning that six thousand people had seen the program.

This was the real beginning of the motion picture theater. First locations were in the downtown areas of the cities. In most instances, the theater was a former store with seats. The first Warner Theater in New Castle, Pennsylvania, had seats rented from the undertaker; if there was a funeral, the show had to suspend operations.

These early films were sold outright by their manufacturer. Edison's standard price was fifteen cents a foot, which meant that it cost $150 to buy a copy. Investment in a projector was about the same amount. With a few hundred dollars, it was possible to rent a store, set it up as a theater, and start to take in nickels. In many instances, the investment was recouped in the first week of operation.

Films were being made in France at this same time, and it was from France that the next important step in movie technique was to come. This was the "magic film" based on stopping the camera. Georges Melies is best known for these films and his *A Trip to the Moon* and *Conquest of the North Pole* remain charming novelties. Edwin V. Porter followed his successful *The Great Train Robbery* with a far more interesting film called *The Dream of a Rarebit Fiend.* Here we have a combination of a story with trick effects—what was later to be called montage photography. Whether Porter copied his work from Melies or whether he came upon the technique at the same time is not important. There began to come a steady flow of films from Selig, from Vitagraph, from Biograph, from Lubin, and from Melies and Pathé Frères in France. Pathé Frères made some of the greatest of the early films, and it is regrettable that there is no knowledge available of the individuals involved. There must have been many talents at work for Pathé.

The story of Faust, which they called *Weird Fancies, The Red Spectre, The Spring Fairy*, and many others rate with the Melies films as true examples of the magic film. *The Enchanted Glasses* shows wine glasses into which wine is poured and girls appear— and from which the girls disappear when the wine is poured out. *Transformation* shows a rose that changes form and out of which comes a small baby. There is an artistry in these early French films that is present only in *The Dream of a Rarebit Fiend* on the American screen.

Other early French films include *The King's Nightmare, The Captain of the Guard*, and *In the Days of Louis XVI*. These films have elaborate settings of castles and highways, with casts of many people actively rushing about. Still other early French films are of travel subjects: *The River Eure, Up the Mountain to Hong Kong, Moscow Clad in Snow, Ruins of Ancient Rome*, and many more.

Still other early French films are said to be the inspiration for the slapstick comedies of Mack Sennett. *A Maniac Juggler, The Travels of a Barrel*, and *An Impractical Journey* are some of these; the technique is of the chase, fast movement, and visual comedy.

Still another contribution of the French was the animated cartoon, the ancestor of Bugs Bunny and Mickey Mouse. *The Hasher's Delirium*, produced in France in 1906, is a combination of an animated cartoon with live action. A man drinks too much, falls asleep, and his dream is enacted entirely by drawings, all of which are a warning against the use of too much alcohol.

It was possible to operate a theater continuously in some locations in 1903, but it was not always easy, and there were many who entered the business in hopes of wealth only to retire quite shortly. There was no steady flow of films available. In locations with a large transient trade, as in Pittsburgh, it was possible to run *The Great Train Robbery* for many months and not to reach a point at which insufficient nickels came in. In smaller places, the novelty soon wore off. New films had to be secured and these were not readily available.

Porter made for Edison *Jack and the Beanstalk* and *The Night Before Christmas*. Lubin refilmed *The Great Train Robbery*, scene for scene, but he also made it "bigger and better," with more people in each scene. Lubin also made a film called *The Bold Bank Robbery* and another called *The Lost Child*. Selig offered *The Dead-wood Stage* and a series of short comedies. The Vitagraph films began to appear. There were also available copies of all of the earlier films, including the famous ones made by Porter just before *The Great Train Robbery*, called *The Life of the American Cowboy* and *The Life of the American Fireman*. Production, however, was geared to the sale of copies of the films to showmen who would travel and exhibit them in different towns as a novelty. The theater with a fixed location had problems. The owner could not endlessly show the same film; he must change his program frequently, yet the cost of buying films for a change of program was prohibitive.

It is at this point that distribution first developed. The owner of a theater in a good permanent location needed to acquire new films either by purchase or by swapping them with someone who had a similar operation in a distant part of the city or in another city. This became the practice. These exhibitors with fixed locations exchanged films. Some of them went into it as a business. This type of business was called a "film exchange." The name has continued.

Men who started in this way include Carl Laemmle, of Universal, Roy and Harry Aitken, John R. Freuler, C. C. Hite of Mutual, and many more. They were first actively interested in the operation of their theater or theaters; they were subsequently interested in the acquisition of films and in the booking of these films to other theaters. First transactions were on a basis of the sale of a film with a credit allowance for an old film traded in on the purchase. Later transactions between smaller theaters and the film exchange men became much simpler. The theater paid a rental for the film. The exchange man bought it, showed it in his own theater or theaters, and rented it out as many times as he could.

Traffic continued in secondhand copies of films for many years after production. In 1910, seven years after production, copies of *The Great Train Robbery* were offered for outright sale at fifteen to twenty-five dollars. Likewise were all of the early films. Some of these were well-worn copies of slight value since they would break and tear and disrupt the show. Others were known as "cold copies," actually reprints, and in such an instance the film was new.

One of the most important men of the early years was George Kleine of Chicago. Kleine Optical had the Chicago agency for the Edison projectors and films. It also had the Biograph agency. Mr. Kleine early appreciated the importance of the European films, and he was the first to import films made by Eclipse and Gaumont of France, and Cines and Ambrosio of Italy. He formed the Kalem

Company, in association with Long and Marion—the name Kalem is a combination made from their initials. Another combination of initials was the "S and A" of Chicago, spelled out "Essanay." The "S" was for George Spoor of Waukegan, Illinois, and the "A" was for Max Aaronson, who went west, used the screen name Gilbert M. Anderson, and made a whole series of western films that featured himself in the role of Broncho Billy.

It was these films, and others like them, that held for the American moviemaker a distinct place in the sun. The French films were far superior in many respects. However, the American cowboy film was distinctive. Broncho Billy's films were actually made at Niles, California, and the background of the West was real. Some of the other Westerns of the era were made at Fort Lee, New Jersey, but the format was American.

We have now reached 1907. Theaters were making sensational money. They opened in the morning, showed until late at night, and there were waiting lines. Since the program lasted only a half hour or less, it was literally possible to take in nickels from several thousand people in a day. Very little of this money reached the studios. A small part of it got to the exchanges in the form of rentals for the films; even less got to the studio, or film manufacturer. There were now eight or more American sources for films, six or more foreign sources represented with agents in the American markets, and many smaller foreign concerns as yet unrepresented in the States.

The exchanges were making money also. The life of a film was long, and even those reels that broke or tore during projection could be patched up and sent out to earn an extra rental.

But the studios were in difficulties. Costs of production were continuously going up. Competition was keen. It was not so easy now to make a film without a regular cast and without a story. The day had long since gone when workers' leaving the Lumiere factory had any interest. Stories that sold well, like the new Broncho Billy films from Essanay, were profitable but even here rebates were needed to bring orders from some exchanges. Cost of film was stable at fifteen cents a foot for new films on release date, but the sale of so-called cold copies a few weeks after release date at discounted prices lowered the returns to the filmmaker. Above all, no return was possible to him on his earlier successes, and no matter how many times a film was shown or how much money it brought in, none of it reached the manufacturer after the initial sale. Great traffic was had in secondhand film copies, and at one time it was estimated that more than 80 percent of the theaters in the country were supplied by "junk film exchanges," film exchanges that did not invest in new copies.

The only incentive to make better films was the hope that more copies would be sold, and the margin of profit of the studio was the difference between the cost of the raw film plus the laboratory cost of manufacture and the selling price. With New York controlled by William Fox, with Philadelphia controlled by Lubin, and with tight control in many areas, the studio was definitely in an unattractive spot. The exhibitor was in a strong bargaining position; movie films were of no interest to a grocery store or a drug store—they could not be bought or sold in the marketplace without a theater. Still other problems came from the ease with which duplicate negatives could be made. It was most difficult to prevent the purchaser of a copy of a film from using it to make a duplicate negative and thereafter from making his own copies without payment of any kind to the studio that had made the film in the first place.

Many films could be made cheaply. One full-length reel was made by an early manufacturer under some such title as *Harry's Hats*. The cast was one man. The action showed him trying on one hat after another and discarding each one. Truly more was needed if the public was to continue to attend the theaters. More elaborate stories meant more time in production, larger casts of actors, higher costs. There was an attempt to compel buyers to accept and pay for every film made by each studio. On this basis, the low cost of a film like *Harry's Hats* could offset the cost of a more elaborate film. However, competition became keen; discount sales, sales on credit with slow payment, and other problems brought the studios to the point of no return.

2

With this situation, which brought all of the American manufacturers together in an association to be known as The Motion
Picture Patents Company, the industry took its first steps toward
stabilization. In brief, patents on projectors, cameras, and films held
by Edison, Biograph, and others were given to the Patents Company. A demand was made for license fees for the right to use film,
camera, or projector. The license fee was small. Theater payments
were only two dollars per week. At this time there were more than
twenty thousand theaters in operation, most of them small store
affairs, so even this modest amount would bring an income of more
than two million dollars a year to the trust, if it could be collected.
It wasn't. Some escaped. But this was not the important purpose of
the Patents Company.

The real strength was to be found in the license agreement,
which everyone who wanted to deal in licensed films had to sign.
This license agreement, with respect to theaters, made it mandatory
to use only licensed films in a licensed theater. Use of an unauthor-
ized film was grounds for immediate cancellation of the license
and refusal to supply any films. All films of this period had plainly
printed on one side of the celluloid the words "Leased for use only
on machines licensed by the Motion Picture Patents Company."
On the other side of the film was the name of the producer, for
example, "Property of Selig Polyscope Company," or "Property of
Thomas A. Edison, Inc.," as the case might be. These words and
the license agreement were the legal basis relied on by the Patents
Company in some sensational activities.

A large part of the money collected as license fees went to en-
forcers, people a later era would call by such names as "goon
squads." These strong-arm men descended on theaters from time

to time demanding to see what films were in use. If any unlicensed films were found, they were seized, carried away, or burned, and the license of the theater was suspended and shipments of films were stopped. Sometimes the theater was closed for good, and the projector taken out and carted away by the agents of the Patents Company. Other times, the offender paid a cash fine, promising to be good henceforth, and he was allowed to reopen.

With all of the American manufacturers in the Patents Company, it was a period of time when control was almost complete. No source existed for films other than these manufacturers. Stocks of films sold previously could be used and a few copies of films made in Europe were available, but the first result of the Patents Company was highly effective.

Individual theaters were one thing; distributors or operators of film exchanges were another. The Patents Company directed its greatest effort toward the film exchanges, which first had to sign an agreement to buy and book only licensed films. After ninety days of use they were to surrender all films so that they could be taken off the market and burned; there was to be an end to the life of a film. This way, new films would be freed from the competition of old ones. A "release date" was established for each film and though copies might reach the exchanges before this date, a heavy fine was assessed if they were given to a theater before this date. Other provisions of the license agreement between the Patents Company and the individual exchanges were detailed, and breach of any one of the many elaborate paragraphs of this agreement was grounds for cancellation of the license and also for the surrender of all films in the exchange.

The Motion Picture Patents Company was quickly followed by the organization of the General Film Company, Inc., a concern that never required any cash in its treasury for its operations and whose stock was owned entirely by the studios. General Film bought out most of the exchanges. Nonvoting preference stock, notes, and possibly some form of bond given by General were the considerations available to the exchange men who accepted its terms for the sale to General of their businesses. The ones who did not accept were soon found to be in default on their license agreement and strong-arm men stepped in to take over their stock of films and to collect the rentals paid by their customers.

The studios continued to invoice the offices of the General

Film Company with the selling price of the new films at the standard rate of fifteen cents a foot. More copies were sold. The sale of cold copies and discounted copies was discontinued. Now for the first time, substantial profits came to the studios that made the films.

Profits made by General Film quickly passed the million-dollar mark and were to reach more than five million dollars in one of their early years. This from the nickelodeon or nickel movie. Even these figures are inaccurate, for substantial profits passed from General Film by the purchase of copies of the films and these payments were shown as expense of operation and taken out of the receipts before any profit was indicated. Receipts from the license fees paid by the theaters also did not get accounted for by General Film but went to the studios as dividends from the Patents Company.

General Film set new policies in the industry. Rental was to be determined by the age of the film. Highest rental was for the use of the film on the first day of release. Rental became less with each day after release. Terms like "Seven-Day Service" and "Fourteen-Day Service" indicated the length of time after release date. After a month of use, films were designated as "thirty-day stuff" and were available at modest rentals. At the end of the second month, films were called "commercial service" and relegated to the small towns and the smallest neighborhood theaters, where they ended their days. They were supposed to go back to the studios to be burned at the end of the third month but some may have been held a little longer.

The producers all became millionaires. Not all of them remained in this classification to the end of their days because show business has a way of turning on its impresarios from time to time. Only one of the pioneer manufacturers was to survive into the 1920s. But they were to have a period of high living and great prosperity.

More detail can be had on "the trust" and all of it is adverse. It was to be broken up by the government in 1914 under the Sherman Act; an examination of the testimony taken in the antitrust proceedings is lurid reading. I am not concerned here with the ethics, or lack of ethics, of the trust. What interests me is what happened after it was formed and how it led to the advancement of the cinema. It is clear to me that without the trust and the methods that it created, the production of more elaborate films could not have come about. Certainly public interest grew steadily as better films were made, and better and more expensive films could never have come from studios that did not have money available to them.

Only one man held out against the trust. He was William Fox. He had a license to buy from the studios for his film exchange, known as Greater New York Film Rental Agency. He resisted in the courts every attempt to cancel his license. He refused to sell his business. He secured an injunction restraining cancellation of his license and compelling delivery of films. Fox had legal manpower and strong political connections; he had theaters in metropolitan New York that brought in a large flow of necessary cash. He was to found Fox Film Corporation before many years had passed.

Others were to hang onto business of a sort as distributors, but everyone except Fox had to turn to other sources for films. Carl Laemmle and Pat Powers produced their own pictures and combined with other independent men to form Universal. Roy and Harry Aitken formed Mutual with C. C. Hite, Kessell and Bauman, and John R. Freuler. These men's initial efforts were concentrated on making films, and they fought pitched battles to keep control of cameras with which to photograph them. At one time, Laemmle's forces fled to Cuba to escape the strong-arm men of the Patents Company. Kessell and Bauman made movies of gangsters, and the casts were real: strong-arm men on the payroll protected the cameras when needed and acted in front of them when things were quiet enough to permit films to be taken. All of these independent studios drew on Europe for raw film, cameras, and equipment, as well as the completed films of European studios that were not in the combine. Although for several years General Film dominated the industry and the independent forces were very weak, indeed, they eventually triumphed.

There was one way in which General Film did not attempt to control the showing of its films: Anyone and everyone who was willing to pay the established rate for films could get them without any reference to any other theater. There was later to be another and even more substantial lever by which the distributor of films could increase the rental payments. This was to be the system known as "protection," or the auctioning of preferential runs whereby one theater would have a film for showing before his competitor could get it.

Competition was keen in the days when several theaters were

located only a block or two apart. Each exhibitor was eager to get films before his competitor. The men in control of General Film either did not realize this fully or they were fully occupied with the activities I have already outlined. Not so with all of their employees.

Control of the booking of films and their shipment from the exchange to the theaters was in the hands of a man known as a booker. Once a contract was signed with a theater that specified the rental to be paid, the actual shipments were made by this man. It was possible to make a donation to this man's favorite charity (himself) and get preferential treatment. If the donation was substantial, it meant that new films went to the theater that contributed it, regardless what the contract called for. If it was really magnificent, it meant that trouble was visited upon competitors of the contributor. They would get old worn-out films. Mistakes would happen frequently. They would get films previously shown by them—"repeaters"—instead of new films as promised. Foreign films made by Pathé, Melies, and the ones released by Kleine were less popular than the American makes. They would show up regularly on the unfortunate competitor's screen while the new, attractive films made by Edison, Vitagraph, Lubin, Selig, and Kalem were exclusively shown at the theater from which the donation came.

One town with twelve small store-shows also had a legitimate theater of substantial size. A very wise individual leased this theater and signed a contract with General Film for programs at the modest rental of fifteen dollars a week, which normally meant films a month or more behind release date. However, the donation to the booker was fifty dollars per week and, as a result, the large theater soon became the only one in town to do business. Its programs were always new and popular; the latest films came to its screen. Competitors frequently had dark screens when a mistake was made in shipping the film and it did not arrive in time. When they did come in they frequently broke, as the copies were old and worn. The availability of foreign films with a complete lack of Westerns did not help matters. Pictures recently shown would return without warning or posters sent in for the front of the theater announcing what was playing would not be for the films that were actually delivered.

Efforts were made to control operations of this kind. Investigators from General Film were kept constantly on the move. When excessive donations were uncovered, the booker and the manager were quickly removed and new employees sent to replace them. Neither the booker nor the manager could walk into his office in the morning and be certain that he would not be visited by someone from New York with authority to demand the bank books, the keys, the records, and his exit. Turnover of manpower was substantial.

In one instance, word got to the management of an exchange that they were being investigated for charitable-donation activities. They did not wait for the next morning. They left at night, taking with them all records. When the investigator walked in, he found an empty office without even an office boy. Calls had to be made to each theater to the effect, "Tell us, please, what you have booked and what rental you pay us." They were, indeed, interesting days on all levels.

The graft and intrigue of these early days may be compared to life on a frontier town where the discovery of gold or other sudden wealth brings in a motley crew. Certainly men came to the motion picture from all sources, and sudden wealth was the lure. The industry in all its branches was as lurid as the story in any of its wildest gangster or cowboy films.

The complete domination of the Patents Company in these early years made possible many excesses. And each excess or injustice was to make more possible the breakdown of the system and the entry of new forces as competitors.

From the standpoint of production, progress was definite and immediate. Sufficient finances were now available to do new and interesting things. This is the era in which Edison made *The Charge of the Light Brigade, Paul Revere's Ride, The Star-Spangled Banner* and *Pickwick.* This also is the period when Edison made *Abraham Lincoln* with Frank McGlynn, who many years later was to play in the John Drinkwater play of the same name. Edison also sent men to film Niagara Falls, Yellowstone Park, and many other scenic or historic spots. Edison was personally interested in the film as an aid to education, and he diverted substantial sums to the filming of pictures that he believed to be of educational value. Furthermore, through his connection with the Patents Company, he insisted that the exchanges buy copies of all of them, whether desired or not, and he insisted that they be shown.

One of the strongest beliefs of Edison, Kleine, and others of the Patents group was that the programs must never be allowed to become stereotyped; there must be variety. Later, when exhibitors were relatively free of domination from the studios and their distribution agencies, they would insist upon the right to select and play "the most popular pictures," and this was responsible for the endless cycle of Westerns, slapsticks, and wronged-girl films that from time to time dominated. The men in control of General felt that it was to the advantage of the industry to have as much variety as possible. Westerns and comedies, of course, but not exclusively.

The classics were drawn on. *Romeo and Juliet* and *As You Like It* were made into films. Tolstoi was filmed by Selig. Ibsen was also produced in films.

In addition to variety, other rules were laid down that could not be deviated from on pain of loss of film service. Three reels of film might be shown for a nickel. Five reels might be shown for a dime. A different program was to be shown in a theater each day. All of these rules had a foundation of good business sense. It was thought that frequent attendance at theaters would decrease if programs were excessively long. Years later, double-feature programs with each movie two hours and longer were to make the theater a weekend affair. In the days of General Film, it was possible to see a movie program any and every night and be fresh the following morning for school or business.

The time limitation—a film must be complete within an arbitrary fifteen-minute length—was to insure variety and the availability of more than one type of entertainment on every program. This was one of the most troublesome rules in the studios. Some stories simply could not be told in this short length. Vitagraph's *As You Like It* simply stretched out to three reels. So did Selig's *Cinderella* and *The Two Orphans*. Griffith held *Enoch Arden* to two reels, but he could not tell the story in any shorter time. They were originally released on different dates as a serial, with the first reel to be shown on one night and the second reel on the following night in the instance of *Enoch Arden*, and over three different nights in the instance of *As You Like It*. The original showings of these pictures were in accord with the rules but later showings ran the complete film at one sitting.

Other films stretched to even longer lengths. *From the Manger to the Cross* simply could not be brought down to a length shorter than five reels; it was withheld from the regular customers and handled as a road attraction in theaters that ordinarily presented stage plays.

3

Hollywood itself was early visited by companies of traveling film players who were looking for new and different locations. The Selig group headed by Hobart Bosworth was the first group to remain, and the Selig studio was established as the first one in California. The fact that California was more than three thousand miles from the goon squads of the Patents Company most certainly was attractive to the early independent forces.

But in these first early years of studio prosperity, Hollywood was only one of many locations—far from Fort Lee, New Jersey— where pictures could be made on locations that were valid and real. George Kleine had a truly worldwide perspective. His Kalem company was to make *From the Manger to the Cross* in the Holy Land and in Egypt. This same company, under the direction of Sidney Olcott, was later to go to Ireland and to make there a series of films. Other locations in which Kalem companies operated included Jacksonville, Florida, New Orleans, Louisiana, and both Glendale and Santa Monica in California, while the original studio at Fort Lee continued to grind out pictures. The New Orleans studio produced *The Confederate Iron Clad*, the story of the *Monitor* and the *Merrimac*. The story of Francis Marion was filmed on many different locations in the South and released as *The Swamp Fox*. Another Kalem company went to Quebec to film *Wolfe and Montcalm* on the Plains of Abraham.

Ten tons of Irish soil were purchased by the Kalem Company and shipped back to the United States. As part of the advertising campaign for the films made in Ireland, this soil was packed into little boxes about two feet square and sent out with the films to the theaters where they were shown. These boxes were placed in front of the theater box office, making it possible to "stand on the auld sod" when you attended the theater. The one great advantage that movies of that day had over the stage of that day was the realism that photography of actual places afforded instead of painted scenery. It was this factor that sparked the runaway hunt for distant and unusual locations.

The series of Broncho Billy films began to issue from a small barn called a studio at Niles, California. Broncho Billy was in all of them with his horse, his girl, and a number of badmen. Sometimes Broncho himself was bad, but he had a heart of gold. If he went wrong, he did it in a spirit of good clean fun. If he stole, it was to get even with some stuffy character, and he probably passed on the stolen loot to someone who needed it. How attractive Robin Hood can be to anyone except his victims.

In *Broncho Billy and the Baby*, the heart of a badman is captured by a small child. In *Why Broncho Billy Left Bear County*, Broncho Billy allows himself to be suspected of the robbery of a stagecoach so that the brother of the girl he loves will not be convicted of the crime. They are separated by many miles, since he is a fugitive. However, a tender message from him reaches her, and she is told that "I am reading the Bible you gave me." He does not kiss the girl at the end of the picture.

The story is told of a small boy who had to face up to a serious operation. He feared the anaesthetic. When his mother told him, "Broncho Billy would not be afraid," he submitted without a murmur. This incident was duly reported to Broncho via one of thousands of fan letters. These early actors reached across the miles and seemed very close to their audiences. No doubt the fact that they appeared in at least one new film each week made this so.

The theaters of this early day were in some respects small neighborhood clubs. Lonely people found it to be the high spot of their day to attend the picture show and to be greeted as a friend by the cashier, the man on the door, and by other regulars. This close rapport between the audience and the shadows on the screen is attested by letters such as the one written by a young crippled girl to Mae Marsh, which told how she and her grandfather, with whom she lived, saved and scrimped from his small pension to be able to see Mae in the Biographs. This is not to say that there was not also widespread patronage from all walks of life and from all types of people. However, "the regulars" were very important. General Film recognized this, and the rules of short programs and daily changes were intended to keep this group loyal.

There was another source from which the new theaters drew, and that was the saloon. The type of man who frequented the saloon for social drinking could be lured away, and so he was—to the neighborhood movie show. Because any woman found in the saloons of that day was morally suspect, it was appreciated by the wives of men who spent their idle hours at the theater. They were able to spend social evenings with their husbands at the theater instead of staying home when he went out. So substantial was the defection from the saloons that the first efforts to establish a censorship of the movies was aided financially by the liquor interests.

This atmosphere of a neighborhood social club was helped by the relatively large staff of employees. There were musicians, often a lone pianist, but from time to time a drummer who was also gifted in abilities with horns, steamboat whistles, bird calls, horses' hooves, and other effects. There was often a soloist who led the audience in singing while song slides were thrown on the screen. Even the smallest theater sometimes had vaudeville. Among the attractions that appeared in movie theaters were the man who went over Niagara Falls in a barrel, a lecturer who conversed with the characters in his travel film of China to the complete amazement of his audience, magicians, escape artists, song and dance men, and assorted fugitives from big-time vaudeville. The movies may have been silent, but the theater was not. It was alive and a very pleasant place to be. Attempts were made to add sound effects from the rear of the screen. Lectures were given on the serious films of the era; indeed, *Jerusalem Delivered*, also known as *The Days of the Crusades*, had a complete lecture that was to be given before and during the presentation.

The short length of most pictures meant that people could drop in any time; the movie that was on the screen when they came in would soon end. They would see the next subject from the beginning. This factor meant that attendance in city theaters benefited from people who had a free hour or less before an appointment or before their train left. Clocks were prominently displayed, and much of the afternoon business of the movie houses was of the drop-in kind.

The character of the audiences is reflected in the films. In general, the films are highly moral. Liquor is unattractive· and primarily so because it takes money away from wives and babies that need it. Broncho Billy's good, but somewhat wild, heart could be touched by the Bible, as mentioned previously. Problems such as child labor, equal suffrage for women, and safety measures in the steel mills were presented from the point of view of the masses.

Yet social scientists should guard against making quick judgments. The quantity of film production quickly became tremendous, and from this vast quantity of film, it is possible to select illustrations that can be used to illustrate any point. For example, it is possible to say that the stereotype of the Negro was unfair and that the film degraded him. Scenes from the early movies can certainly be secured that illustrate this. However, if the complete film is shown, it well may be part of a slapstick comedy in which every character, both Negro and Caucasian, is degraded and made funny. Pies were thrown in the faces of society dowagers as well as in the faces of Negro butlers.

The economics of the industry was simple and produced profits. The exchanges took everything that the studios made. They had to because General Film was owned by the studios. The theaters took whatever General Film chose to give them. They had to because there was no other source. The same price was paid for each film and there was no increase in cost for the films that had a higher budget than ordinary.

The Broncho Billy films were the most popular of the early ones made by the Essanay Company. To increase its income, more and more films were made each week, and the exchanges and the theaters were required to take them all. A comedy company at Niles ground out Western comedies, called "the Snakeville comedies," on the same Western locations used in the Broncho Billy films. Other Essanay films were produced in the Chicago studios. Still another company of Essanay players established a studio at Ithaca, New York. It was from this company that Francis X. Bushman became known as one of the first and greatest of all movie stars.

The Vitagraph had John Bunny in a series of comedies that would complement the Broncho Billy films and, like them, be a weekly affair. Bunny was a fat man with an odd face. His companion in most of his films was Flora Finch, a woman who was tall and extremely thin and angular. The appearance of both in the opening scene was the signal for laughter to begin. Sometimes they were husband and wife, and Flora was severe with Bunny's efforts to escape her clutches. Sometimes they were sweethearts and Flora was coy. Other films were made by Vitagraph, of which the best known featured Maurice Costello and Florence Turner. The entire company of Vitagraph players went on to fame as movie stars. Norma Talmadge and her sister, Constance, came to Vitagraph from Erasmus Hall High School in Brooklyn and were later to be among the best known of the stars. Lillian Walker, the girl with the dimples; Hughie Mack, a man even fatter than Bunny; Clara Kimball Young; Anita Stewart; Earle Williams; Antonio Moreno; William Duncan; and many many more started in the early Vitagraph plays. Vitagraph was among the first film producers to make more elaborate and longer films than the ones shown at the time. Although its greatest profits came from the Bunny films and similar inexpensive ones, they made *As You Like It, A Tale of Two Cities, The Deerslayer*, and, a few years later, a film called *My Official Wife* in which Leon Trotsky made an appearance.

The human equation here is interesting. The official of Vitagraph were Smith, Blackton, and Rock, and they were sufficiently interested in getting a buck to be part and parcel of the Motion Picture Patents Company, with its elaborate system of control of the industry. (Blackton took on the title of "commodore" and bought a yacht.) At the same time, they could and did produce films that cost far more than the Bunny comedies, and they sold them at exactly the same price to the exchanges. It is entirely proper to say that a small part of the profits of the Bunny films was diverted away from dividends and used to make *As You Like It* and the rest of the more expensive releases.

Kalem's source of bread and butter income came from a series of comedies produced by Marshall Neilan, which featured Mr. Neilan and Ruth Roland. Many of these were made at Glendale and Santa Monica. The eastern studio at Fort Lee produced a series of films with Alice Joyce and Tom Moore that likewise were consistently profitable. It was Kalem, however, as previously indicated, that spread so far afield with its foreign location filmings. *From the Manger to the Cross* certainly returned tremendous dividends on its investment, since it did not go to the nickelodeon theaters but, instead, went the route of the larger legitimate stage theaters. However, films such as *A School for Scandal, Wolfe and Montcalm*, and *The Swamp Fox* went out the regular way and did not return a penny more to Kalem than did its least expensive films.

With a constant supply of new and more interesting films available, attendance increased at the theaters, and more of them were opened. Demand grew for more and more releases. At one time during the nickelodeon period, six films were made each week by such studios as Vitagraph, Lubin, and Selig, while five different pictures were made by Edison, Kalem, Essanay, and Biograph. All of these films reached the theaters through General Film. To them were added the foreign films of George Kleine, Pathé films, and those made by Melies. Although Pathé and Melies were French companies, they opened studios in the United States and offered American-made films as well as foreign ones. The Pathé studios were in New Jersey; the Melies studio at one time was in Arizona and at another time in Santa Paula, California. At one time during the nickelodeon period, Melies closed his California studio and charted a large ship for a world cruise. It left California with a company of actors, cameramen, technicians, and laboratory equipment and went across the Pacific with film production "on location" in Hawaii, Japan, Samoa, Australia, and New Zealand. These films were not successful and did not bring in the money to Melies that would have come from potboilers, but they are another indication that money was not the sole interest of all early moviemakers and proof that some of them were endowed with genuine creativity.

As a result of the increased demand and accelerated release schedules, lax control was permitted by studio top officials. This is best illustrated at Biograph, although the same general system was in effect at all studios. At Biograph, individual men were delegated authority to make one picture each week and all details were left to them. D. W. Griffith headed one such Biograph group; and Mack Sennett headed another Biograph group; although these are the names best remembered, they are but two out of five or more that made the Biographs.

Griffith's first films were made in New York and were fully approved by the Biograph management as well as by the public. Although they were better films than most of the films of that day, the quality was achieved inexpensively by the use of new techniques such as the close-up, the moving camera, and the flashback. Moreover, pictures such as *The New York Hat, The God Within, The Unwelcome Guest*, and *A Stranger Returns* were not more expensive than other films of their era, but they benefited from the superior technique of Griffith, his intense devotion to detail, and his great willingness to work long overtime hours without putting any charge for this on the cost sheets. They benefited also from the collection of players that included Mary Pickford, Florence

Lawrence, Lillian and Dorothy Gish, Mae Marsh, Blanche Sweet, Henry B. Walthall, Arthur Johnson, Lionel Barrymore, Jack Pickford, and Linda Arvidson. Were these players really the best in the industry of their day? Or did Griffith's direction make them appear so? At any event, the Biograph films were the unquestioned leaders of the films of the nickelodeon. As I said, the cost of the Biograph films was not greater than the cost of the films of any of the other studios that produced for General Film, but their receipts were greater, for they sold more copies. There was a demand for the opportunity to display a poster that said "Biograph Tonight," and it was enough to assure capacity.

It was under this system that Griffith was eventually permitted to go wild and spend money without immediate control. He was allowed to take a company of players to California, and at Malibu he produced *Enoch Arden*. The story simply would not fit into the time format of one reel. Two were made. Upon the delivery of the completed film to the Biograph offices, it was released on two different days as a serial or continued story. Griffith was told not to do this again, and he did not disobey until a later trip to California when he made *The Massacre*, which grew from one reel to two, and *The Battle of Elderbush Gulch*, which grew into a two-reeler. These things were overlooked, however, because *The Battle, Iola's Promise*, and other films made at the same time were kept within the one-reel length. A little eccentricity could be excused in a man like Griffith who made Biograph's best films. Yet the two-reelers did not satisfy him completely; he began work on a film called *Judith of Bethulia*, which stretched into many reels. Every player under his control was drafted to appear, such as Blanche Sweet, who was Judith, and Henry B. Walthall and Mae Marsh. Elaborate battle scenes were staged.

It was possible to do many things with cost sheets when the business office was three thousand miles away. Extra sums went on the sheets for the one-reelers. Cost sheets for *Judith* never did get sent out. This was a system of necessary dishonesty best understandable to a creative mind. The picture *Judith* simply had to be made. It was, and when the company returned to New York with it, it was screened for the officials of Biograph, to their complete disgust. Griffith was discharged without delay and *Judith*, the offending film, was sent to a dark corner of the Biograph vault, where it remained for several years.

Mack Sennett, the other Biograph producer with the right to

be called a genius, did not disobey the head office. This was because all of his films were made in New York, and he had no opportunity to innovate. Sennett's films, which outsold all other Biographs, benefited from his ability to edit them sharply and to provide the sense of comedy that was his inimitable gift. They were, however, made at budget cost. In time, he too left Biograph, probably lured away by the promise of more money and the opportunity to make films in California.

With the departure of Griffith and Sennett, the Biograph officials were left without headaches, but they were also left without distinctive films to sell. The other directors who closely obeyed orders as to cost had ideas that were no less mediocre than the cost sheets. Biograph was to be the first of the pioneer companies to wither away and die. Ironically, its last income was to come from the reprinting of the short Griffith and Sennett films and from the sale of *Her Condoned Sin*, which was the title placed upon Griffith's *Judith of Bethulia* at the time of its last release.

There were films in production in every studio literally waiting to be born in a length greater than the standard of the nickelodeon. The theme and story simply could not be compressed. Before we discuss some of these situations, we must reflect a little on the growth of the independent distributors and theaters. While the trust was effective in a theoretical way in its plans, there were men in theaters and in exchanges who simply would not lay down and play dead. Carl Laemmle was one of them. He got a camera and made a film, *Hiawatha*, and it was every bit as good as the product of the trust companies. He bought films from every source open to him, and his offices, under the title of Laemmle Film Service, stretched through the midwest from Chicago to Omaha, to Minneapolis, to Kansas City, to Des Moines and Sioux City. He found films in England and elsewhere that could be purchased from studios that had no affiliation with the Patents Company. He was able to sell copies of his *Hiawatha* film in England and in his native Germany. It is simply impossible to assess the native intelligence, the tremendous energy, and the driving force of this man. He generated the finances from which grew the most successful of the early film companies from his own activities. Universal was literally a growth situation whose roots go back to the White Front Theater in Chicago, the Laemmle Film Service, and the just plain guts of a fighter.

S. S. Hutchinson and John R. Freuler, under pressures similar to those that faced Laemmle, organized the American Film Manufacturning Company and sent a company of players to California, where they filmed a series of weekly Western releases similar to the ones made by Broncho Billy for Essanay. Their star was J. Warren Kerrigan, who, toward the end of his career, was to appear in one of the greatest feature-length Western films. His first films were one-reelers, and they had the scenery of southern California.

Still other independent distributors were Kessell and Bauman who with their Eagle Film Exchange in New York were suspended from supply by General Film. They did not close. They got a camera and a man to operate it and posed for pictures in which they themselves appeared with the help of any other people who might be handy. Their first films were rented out quickly and money came in from which many more were to be made. An unsavory background of bookmaking and illicit political connections appears in comments on Kessell and Bauman; they were able to get strong-arm men when they were needed; they did not flinch from direct pitched battles with General Film agents or competitors. It was to Kessell and Bauman that Mack Sennett went when he left Biograph, and it was with funds that they supplied from their Eagle Film Exchange that he left with his small company for California to make Keystone comedies. It was from Kessell and Bauman that the Aitken brothers were later to get needed funds in their days of trial with Triangle. Thomas H. Ince, one of the great early producers, was to make films for Kessell and Bauman and to use their initials "KB" to bring them to the screen.

The independents drew strength, the one from the other. Laemmle took Freuler's American Film Company's movies for his Laemmle Film Service and was glad to get them, as he also was glad to get anything and everything released by Kessell and Bauman. At the same time, Freuler's greatest strength lay in Milwaukee and other parts of Wisconsin, where he operated many theaters as well as a film exchange known as Western Film Supply. So strong was Freuler's control of his immediate area that the trust met its first defeat in Wisconsin, and more theaters in that state showed independent films than any other.

Harry Aitken, with interests in exchanges and in studios, was greatly helped by his brother, Roy, who very early in his career established a base in London from which sales could be made of films produced by the Aitkens or any of their associates and from which supplemental British and continental releases could be secured when needed.

All of these early independent men worked together against the trust, and then also against each other as the winds of business changed. Stories of intrigue would rival the best gangster pictures of the day. Ex-Buffalo policeman Pat Powers was intrenched in Buffalo and Cleveland with his Victor Service. The early association of Pat Powers with Carl Laemmle led to a battle in which Powers threw the company books out the window down to Broadway where they were snatched and run off with by a faithful Powers employee. At one time, Powers held up production at Universal by refusing to sign his name to checks that required two signatures—his and Laemmle's.

Pitched battles between rival gangs of strong-men took place at the KB studios near Malibu in California, when they attempted to withdraw from a distribution contract with Laemmle. Cameras were seized and broken by strong-arm goon squads from the Patents Company. Along with the wilder side of the business, there were court appearances. The Latham Loop on which the Motion Picture Patents Company depended to uphold the validity of the patents on cameras was held to be invalid. Investigations by the Department of Justice threw a measure of fear into the Patents Company, and although General Film did not feel the weight of the Sherman Act officially until 1914, it had begun to be less offensive in its operation several years before that. The goon squads were withdrawn, and independent films were permitted to be shown in theaters on the same program with licensed films.

In all the excitement of the battles between General Film and the independents, William Fox was absent from the spectacular fighting. His Greater New York Film Rental Company did not handle independent films. He did not enter into independent production during the time that he forced General Film to deliver licensed films to his exchanges and his theaters. After the dissolution decree in 1914, he organized Box Office Attractions, and he began his own production of films as well as the distribution of many independent and foreign films.

4

Fascinating as are the details of the struggles of these early years, they must give way to an exposition of their effect on the industry. There were some fifty or more independent films released regularly each week in 1914 and an equal number of licensed, or trust, films. This was a sufficient quantity of films, so that different programs could be given in each of four different theaters. Customers in a neighborhood had a choice of program. Since the programs were short, still held to the hour or hour and a half limits established by General, real movie addicts could take in programs offered at more than one theater, especially on weekends and holidays. Many of them did. Going to the movies for the fans of that era could mean seeing the Universal films at the Bijou, the Mutual films at the Gem, and the General films at the Lyric.

All of this created a demand for stepped-up production, and production jobs could be had for the asking. A man appeared at the Keystone studios in Edendale, California, and told Mack Sennett that his name was Pathé Lehrman; that he was a distant relative of the Pathé Frères of France; and that he had helped them make films. On the strength of this story, he was put to work. Similar stories can be told of almost all studios. Men were entrusted with budgets for the films of the day on the slightest of experiences, and some of them turned out good films. Actors graduated to directors and producers. One of the first of these actors was Hobart Bosworth, who headed the first Selig company to go to California, where he made a series of films, truly the first to be made in California.

Production costs of these days were not high. Everyone who worked in a studio was an employee and belonged to the studio body and soul. Overtime was not imagined. Work started in the early morning and continued until the picture was finished. Frank Mayo, an early star at Selig, earned a salary of $100 per week, which was high for that day. On Monday, he would report to be directed in a film of which he was the star. If this film was finished before the end of the week, he was not released from his obligation to Selig. He must report every morning and be willing to appear as a bank clerk, a police officer, a man in a crowd, or any other part in which he was needed as an extra or bit player. Selig had the same system as Swift Packing: "We use everything but the squeal."

The best illustration of this system is found in *The Knockout*, a Keystone comedy made as a Fatty Arbuckle comedy. The first scenes find Fatty broke in a small town where he is forced to fight a champion prizefighter in the hopes of getting his hands on the cash promised to anyone who would stay in the ring for one round with the champ. The ring scene is the big scene. It takes place on the stage of a theater. To fill the theater seats with an audience, everyone on the Keystone lot was called in: Mack Sennett walks across the set; Mack Swain sits in a box and flashes back and forth on the action on the stage, and Swain's expressive eyes are one of the best parts of the picture; Charlie Chase, Harry McCoy, Slim Summerville sit in the audience; a brief flash of Chester Conklin appears; the bit part of the referee in the fight scenes is played by Chaplin, then just starting his career at Keystone but still a star in his own productions. A riot breaks out and the Keystone Kops are called in for a chase ending. This chase crosses the high society set then being used for *Tillie's Punctured Romance*.

This production, *Tillie's Punctured Romance*, is another example of the film that simply could not be compressed into its planned short length. Although it was made for Mutual as a Keystone two-reeler and probably financed by them on some such system of mixed-up cost sheets as Griffith used at Biograph, it ended up in the hands of Alco, the company from which grew the Metro of Metro-Goldwyn-Mayer, and was their first source of income. Sennett was to do some odd things during his career as producer. Once he escaped the close scrutiny of the cost-conscious auditors at Biograph, he went as wacky and unpredictable as Griffith. He simply could not see why cost sheets were important. Many of his comedies, however, were made at very little cost. Analysis of the Chaplin Keystones will show that they were made within a week or less; that they had no sets that required effort to construct or to film;

and that most of the action was simple in the extreme. Yet in later years Sennett permitted his gag men to spend thousands of dollars on some breakaway effect that would flash on the screen for a second or two, or he would allow days to be spent on scenes with children and animals that at most took less than a minute of screen time. Other ways in which his costs went up was to film a scene several times, print all the takes, look at them, and then discard the entire bunch.

Griffith's films, when he left Biograph to go with Harry Aitken, were supposed to be one- and two-reelers in the Biograph manner. They were. A whole series of Reliance and Majestic films were made by Griffith after he left Biograph. Some of them bore his own personal stamp; some were made by Christy Cabanne and others under the more or less relaxed "supervision" of the master. Griffith's first attention in the Mutual days was on the production of feature films that were to be turned out at the same time as the shorter films. Here the concept of the feature film was fully shared by the Aitkens, but they were cost conscious, as they well had to be. Griffith's salary, the highest in the industry at that period, simply had to be reflected in a lot of film. Feature films made by him at this time included *Home Sweet Home, The Battle of the Sexes, The Floor Below*, and *The Escape*; they were good workmanlike films made on proper budgets. It was not until he began *The Clansman* that he was carried away with a film that simply could not be done with the money available. Salaries were charged up against other releases. Actors were assigned to short regular releases that were ground out in a day, then for the balance of the week the actors went back to *The Clansman*. The production of *The Clansman* was to unbalance Mutual, make profound changes in the industry, and to endure for generations as "the first great picture." But at the time of its production, it was an unplanned affair that, like Topsy, just grew.

Other pictures were also "just growing" at this time. Selig had a film called *The Spoilers* that ran for two hours, which simply did not fit with its one- and two-reel releases. It featured William Farnum, Tom Santschi, and Kathryn Williams in a story of the Alaskan gold rush by Rex Beach. The fight between Farnum and Santschi that climaxed the film is said to be the greatest ever filmed.

Vitagraph was having the same problem. *His Official Wife*, a film on life in Russia under the czars in which Leon Trotsky had a small part, simply grew to feature length. It could not be choked off into a two- or even a three-reel length. Other pictures that grew at Vitagraph included *The Juggernaut, The Island of Regeneration,* and *A Million Bid.* Since these films simply did not fit into the release schedules of General Film, Vitagraph leased and operated a theater on Broadway in which they were first shown.

We must now survey distribution. It was confined for the most part to small theaters of the store show or nickelodeon type. It was dedicated to the daily change of program and with the program held to a modest length.

The demise of the strictly short film was a worldwide affair. Pictures were being made in Italy that provided entertainment for an entire evening. Programs in Rome and Paris were given in large theaters, such as the Gaumont Palace, with orchestras, singers, and stage prologues. Admission prices for these films were in accord with the scale charged for the legitimate stage. George Kleine was in touch with Europe, and he brought the first of the great Italian films to this country. *Homer's Odyssey,* historically the first, in 1912, was shown in a legitimate theater on Broadway and was the first movie to get critical reviews in the New York press. It was followed in 1914 by *Quo Vadis,* best known of all the Cines films imported by Kleine. Others included *Julius Caesar, The Last Days of Pompeii,* and *Spartacus.* Showings were arranged in such cities as Chicago, Boston, Philadelphia, and Washington; George Kleine hired experienced managers of road-show attractions and used the same kind of publicity given to the best stage plays of their day. Tours were undertaken to reach out to every city in the country, and so great was the demand for these attractions that Kleine was able to ask for and get as much as 90 percent of the box office receipts where his films appeared. None of these films reached the movie houses of that day. They were offered only where a standard legitimate theater was available, and while such theaters were at that time widely available, there were great gaps in the landscape where the Kleine films did not appear.

It was into this climate that there came plans to build large theaters for the presentation of motion pictures. The Strand in New York was the first. It was followed by a Strand in Buffalo and by other large theaters. Each such theater was to offer the best in feature-length films, with a program of added attractions to embellish and add class to the affair. A large orchestra with pipe organ to accompany the films was the first essential. It was considered most important to have a surrounding program of suitable short films: The newsreel was a must; to this must be added both a cartoon and a comedy, preferably a Keystone comedy; further embellishment came from a travel film. In the instance of the news and travel films, musical accompaniment was important. Selection of the travel films would be as often as possible in keeping with the locale of the feature picture. Singers and musicians were offered on the stage with elaborate stage settings that related to the theme of the feature picture.

Overnight, the feature era was born. To the several films that had fought for birth, there were added many made directly as feature films. Adolph Zukor and Jesse L. Lasky had been making feature-length films, and these were available to the presentation theaters very quickly. First of the Zukor films, *Queen Elizabeth*, with Sarah Bernhardt, had gone to the nickelodeons with the blessing of General Film. However, Zukor's future films were to go out as Paramount Pictures, and they were to dominate the industry. Carl Laemmle, with his quick grasp of essentials and his intense devotion to every detail of the business, was to find a lucky accident in a batch of films that came in from his studios at Fort Lee. It was another film that had refused to stay within the limits of the one- and two-reelers. Laemmle called it *Traffic in Souls*, since it dealt with the white slave racket and was a warning to girls to beware of the perils of the big cities. This minor film was every bit as important in its way as the great Kleine films. While *Julius Caesar* brought the carriage trade to the legitimate theaters of the day, *Traffic in Souls* brought out everybody. Lines stood for hours in front of the theaters where this epic appeared. The latter film was truly more educational than Edison's *Lincoln*, because it was popular and thus emulated. Pictures such as *What Became of My Children?*, *The Drug Terror*, and *Damaged Goods* were to follow and to bring the term "visual education" into the language.

There were at first two distinct types of large theaters offering feature motion pictures. The first, like the Strand in New York, was dedicated primarily to the feature film, which was its main attraction; orchestras, stage attractions, and other features were added, but they were supplements. The other type of theater that offered feature pictures was the large vaudeville house, which now included a full-length feature picture on its bill instead of a short one as a chaser. These theaters were perfectly willing to subordinate the entire bill to a strong motion picture, and if one was available to them they billed it as the top attraction and subordinated even the actors to the picture in the billing and advertising.

Both of these types of theaters had one common effect: They eliminated many of the smaller theaters. The opening of one large-capacity theater was the signal for several smaller ones in the neighborhood of the new theater to close. The small theaters that did manage to keep running were to get less and less patronage and to have to make adjustments to the new era. For a few years, short-length films of the type that the small theaters had found profitable continued to be produced, but they grew fewer and fewer and finally vanished, except for the slapstick comedies, the travel films, the cartoons, and the newsreels. Short dramatic films simply could not be found. Stars that formerly appeared in them were in demand for the "bigger and better" feature pictures. No longer was Mae Marsh available on a weekly basis to her little crippled friend and her grandfather. Instead she was to make four or three or two or one picture each year. The large theaters took the idea of music and live-stage attractions and improved upon it. This was their strength. Capacities of several thousand seats, coupled with programs that ran from morning until late evening, meant that receipts could run to many thousands of dollars in a week at the picture palaces.

Before we leave the era of the short film, it is pleasant to think a bit of Edwin Thanhouser, the stock company man from Milwaukee who went to New Rochelle to establish an early independent studio.

The Thanhouser studio was the individual operation of Mr. Thanhouser from its inception until 1914 when he retired and turned over the studio to C. C. Hite. It was under the management of Mr. Hite that the very successful serial, *The Million Dollar Mystery*, was made. Mr. Hite's death in an auto accident brought Mr. Thanhouser back from a European vacation to resume operation of the studio, and he remained at his post for three years more. During this time he made such feature productions as *Fires of Youth*, with Jeanne Eagels, and a series of filmings of such classics as *Silas Marner, The Mill on the Floss, The Flight of the Duchess, The Vicar of Wakefield, King Lear,* and *The Man Without a*

Country. He also continued production of short films during these years. Among them, the interesting and unusual film *The Spirit of Audubon* was taken in the bird islands off the coast of Louisiana where President Theodore Roosevelt had earlier created a bird reserve. The pictures that Thanhouser made with Marguerite Snow, James Cruze, Florence LaBadie, Jeanne Eagels, Charlotte Walker, Irving Cummings, and many others were by no means restricted to the classics and included pictures that were as sensationally successful as those of any studio.

As the cost of production rose, it became more and more difficult to operate a small studio on an individual basis. Marguerite Snow was given a very large salary to leave Thanhouser and go to the new Metro Company. Thanhouser, himself, was offered a most substantial amount to leave his own studio and to go with Paramount as a producer. He decided instead to retire. The studio was sold, the pictures were sold, and Mr. Thanhouser retired to his home on Long Island where he lived for many years. He was the only one of the pioneer producers to accept gracefully the end of the early era of movie making and to refuse to take part in the mad scramble for "bigger and better" feature pictures made on higher and higher cost sheets. James Cruze was to go with Paramount as a director and to make *The Covered Wagon, Old Ironsides, The Pony Express*, and many other fine films. Irving Cummings was to direct a series of very successful films for many years thereafter.

A LA CONQUÊTE DU MONDE

scène vécue
PAR
PATHÉ FRÈRES

HUMOR IN MINIATURE
Starewitch Marionette Film

ORIGINAL DRAWING BY GEORGE MELIES FOR "A TRIP TO THE MOON" (1902)

CINÉMATOGRAPHE LUMIÈRE

The first motion picture poster. It advertised showings at the Grand Cafe, 1896.

The early films experimented with marionettes, animation, and trick shots. *Bottom left:* One of the first moving pictures was of employees leaving the Lumière film factory in France. The moon with the telescope eye was for Melies's *A Trip to the Moon.*

Scene from "JACK AND THE BEANSTALK."

EDISON FILMS

TUESDAY, JANUARY 16th
"JACK AND THE BEANSTALK"
CAST.

Jack...Gladys Hulette
His Mother...Miriam Nesbitt
The Giant...Harry Eytinge
The Giant's Wife...Gertrude Clarke
The Fairy...Gertrude McCoy

A fairy tale, as familiar in the homes as a household word, unfolding the adventures of Jack, his triumphant return from the mystic height of the beanstalk with the giant's ill-gotten treasures. The photographic work, in showing the size of the giant and his wife, is little short of wonderful.

"Vanity Fair"
Mrs. Fiske Gives Screen Interpretation of Becky Sharp in
Edison Production of Thackeray's Novel.

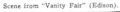

Scene from "Vanity Fair" (Edison).

Edison Players in England.

Seated in front are Charles Brabin, director; Miss Miriam Nesbitt, Marc MacDermott and Miss Bessie Bannon, secretary to Mr. H. G. Plimpton. The rest of the group are English players who have been working with the company regularly. Among the productions made by this company are "The Coast Guard's Sister," "Keepers of the Flock," "Flood Tide," "The Stroke of the Phoebus Eight," "A Daughter of Romany," "The Foreman's Treachery," and others. Both Mr. Brabin and Mr. MacDermott are of English nativity. Miss Nesbitt has also played several engagements on the English stage.

Thomas Alva Edison *(top left)* in his film studio. *Top right, moving clockwise:* A program clip of *Jack and the Beanstalk;* Frank McGlynn, who appeared in the Edison masterpiece *Abraham Lincoln;* Edison players in England; and a scene from *Vanity Fair,* taken from a magazine review.

The Pied Piper of Hamelin

From a poem by Robert Browning

A FANCIFUL and delightful illustration of the old folk tale in which the Pied Piper lures first the rats and then the children of Hamelin town into the side of the mountain.

Hamelin town was infested with a plague of rats. The mayor and corporation, at their wits ends, held a meeting to determine what should be done. Just as they had decided that their situation was hopeless, a stranger in a pied robe entered—

And "Please your honors," said he, "I'm able,
By means of a secret charm, to draw
All creatures living beneath the sun,
That creep or swim or fly or run,
After me so as you never saw!
And I chiefly use my charm
On creatures that do people harm,
The mole and toad and newt and viper;
And people call me the Pied Piper——"
"I eased in Asia and Nizam
Of a monstrous brood of vampyre-bats;
And as for what your brain bewilders,
If I can rid your town of rats
Will you give me a thousand guilders?"
"One? Fifty thousand!" was the exclamation
Of the astonished Mayor and Corporation.
Into the street the Piper stepped,
Smiling first a little smile,
As if he knew what magic slept
In his quiet pipe the while——;

e played a strange weird tune on his pipe and the
and followed him down to
d of them! The piper having
t, asked the mayor for the
The mayor, who was a can-
e rats couldn't come to life
ders. This did not suit the

THE GREAT TRAIN ROBBERY (1903)

DREAM OF THE RAREBIT FIEND

The first film to use double exposure:— examples of what Hollywood calls montage

Sail over the roof tops of New York:—See devils climb out of a chafing dish:—watch the magic of a flying bed and disappearing furniture.

THE NIGHT BEFORE CHRISTMAS" (EDISON 1904)

More films from the Edison studios. John Rice and May Irwin in *The Kiss,* a one-minute film that was nothing more than a closeup; *The Pied Piper of Hamelin; The Night Before Christmas; The Great Train Robbery;* and *Dream of the Rarebit Fiend,* the first film to use double exposure, or what Hollywood later called montage.

EDISON

This sheet is a composite taken from two of the original Edison-Kleine advertisements for the film.

THE MIDNIGHT RIDE OF PAUL REVERE

Retold after the famous poem by HENRY W. LONGFELLOW.

Of all the characters of our Revolutionary period, none is more endeared to young and old than that of Paul Revere, whose exploit has been immortalized by Longfellow so effectively that the lines of the poem and the incidents portrayed are graven more deeply, perhaps, upon the average American mind than any other character or exploit of our American history.

The action throughout this film is finely sustained and many of the scenes, including Revere's house, that of Hancock, the wall at Lexington, where the first shots were fired, were all taken on the exact historical spots where the original action took place.

This is a film that will stir the hearts and minds of young and old and should be met with a tremendous welcome throughout the entire country.

*T*HE historic ride of Paul Revere, taken on the actual scenes of his ride. The captions are the lines of Longfellow's poem.

This familiar poem, which immortalizes a great incident in the history of our country, is visualized in a film tale that is historically accurate. To effect this, the best sources have been consulted, and no expense has been spared in the reconstruction of the period of 1775.

We see Paul Revere urge his friend to hang a lantern aloft in the belfry as soon as the British are marching out of the town; we see him standing on the opposite shore waiting for the signal; we see the signal flash on his vision; we see him spring at once to his saddle, scurry away, "a shape in the moonlight, a bulk in the dark," to spread the alarm to every town and hamlet of Middlesex.

The fate of a nation was riding that night. We see the farmers, roused from their beds by his knock at their door, seize their weapons, take hurried leave of their dearest, and rush forth to do and die. We witness the furious combat between the British Regulars and the farmers who, under the impetus of patriotism, down their better-trained foe.

Meanwhile, impatient to mount and ride,
Booted and spurred, with a heavy stride
On the opposite shore walked Paul Revere.

And lo! as he looks, on the belfry's height
A glimmer, and then a gleam of light!
He springs to the saddle, the bridle he turns,
But lingers and gazes till full on his sight
A second lamp in the belfry burns!

So, through the night rode Paul Revere;
And so through the night went his cry of alarm
To every Middlesex village and farm—
A cry of defiance and not of fear,
A voice in the darkness, a knock at the door,
And a word that shall echo forevermore!

THE CAST

PAUL REVERE	AUGUSTUS PHILLIPS
LIEUTENANT GRAVES	RICHARD TUCKER
GENERAL GAGE	HARRY LINSON
LIEUTENANT HENRY	YALE BENNER
DR. WARREN	BENJAMIN F. MEARS

A composite of two Edison-Kleine advertisements for *The Midnight Ride of Paul Revere.*

"FOR THE HONOR OF THE 7th"

BRONCHO FEATURE   Wednesday, Oct. 2

Thrilling, Spectacular, Military Subject

One Reel

A lieutenant and a captain love the same girl. In a sensational battle with the Indians the soldiers are hard pressed. The lieutenant persuades him to order a retreat, though reinforcements are rushed to the rescue. The captain is court-martialed and the lieutenant turns against him. Discharged, the captain discovers the dual life of the lieutenant, and with bearded face secures employment as a scout. During a battle the lieutenant is fatally wounded and in a dramatic scene confesses his duplicity and the wrong he has done the captain, who is reunited with the girl he loves.

Broncho Motion Picture Co.

"The Grey Sentinel"

Grand Spectacular Military and Naval Production

Wonderful Battle Scenes—The Sinking of the Blockade-Running Vessel.

The Death Struggle Between the Soldiers on the Lighthouse.

A Powerful Dramatic Story of Love and War, Romance and Sensation

Hal Peters, a loyal Southern boy, loves Grace Carson, daughter of the lighthouse keeper. His rival, John Adams, is an officer at West Point. When the war breaks out Adams ostensibly resigns his commission and enters the Southern army, but is secretly a spy for the Union forces. The Confederates plan to land a cargo from a blockade runner, and Adams notifies the Union soldiers, who plant a cannon at the water's edge and sink the ship. Peters discovers Adams' treachery, and in a terrific hand-to-hand struggle Peters is hurled over the cliff, and is found and revived by the lighthouse keeper, who takes a shot at Adams and brings him down as he is escaping in a rowboat.

Florence Vidor as Barbara Frietchie

For the Honor of the 7th and *The Grey Sentinel* were produced by Thomas H. Ince for Kessell and Bauman. This was the same company for which Mack Sennett made his Keystone comedies. Shown above with Ince and Sennett are some of the stars of the California studio.

A composite of films from the Selig studios in California. Hobart Bosworth is pictured below Selig; Frank Mayo is to the right of Bosworth. The jungle scene is from *Thor, the Lord of the Jungle* with Kathlyn Williams.

A KLEINE-CINES FEATURE OF UNUSUAL POWER

"The Sign of the Black Lily"

(In Two Reels)   For Release Tuesday, Sept. 2, 1913

Essentially a Dramatic Story combining a delightful tale of adventure with those wonderful stage settings for which house of Cines is famous.

You will like "The Sign of the Black Lily." Full of adventure, crowded with unexpected situations of splendid power, assisted by those most remarkable of stage mechanics, you find a new thrill in the charm of this delightful two-part subject.

How a wary, old white-haired favorite of the clubs and drawing-rooms is exposed as the leader of the "Black Lily" gang — how an enterprising detective wormed his way into the foul heart of the most vicious and corrupt organization in all Paris — how, by finding secret buttons, walls moved, floors disappeared revealing strange hiding places of the gang. What happened to the police — the valiant fight against overwhelming odds — the dramatic unmasking of the sleek villian in his own reception room crowded with guests — who little suspected his real character — all makes a film delightful for its strong situations, convincing acting and clever story.

George A. Kleine, of Chicago, was one of the first filmmakers to import foreign films. *The Sign of the Black Lily* by Cines of Italy is an example.

The Last Days of Pompeii, Antony and Cleopatra, and *Homer's Odyssey* were three more films from Cines brought to this country by George Kleine. Films such as these were shown in legitimate theaters at legitimate-theater prices, while U.S. film companies were making one-reelers for the nickelodeons. *Homer's Odyssey* was the first film to be reviewed on the theatrical pages of the *New York Times.*

The Broncho Billy films from Essanay Studios in Niles, California, helped to make the Western the quintessential American film.

Kalem Housewarming.

New Studio at Jacksonville, Fla., Scene of Much Merry-Making—A Society Event.

THE elite of Jacksonville society, the most prominent municipal officials and the members of the Lubin and Edison companies located in that cty were the guests of the Kalem players at a housewarming party given in celebration of the completion of the new enclosed Kalem studio, on Saturday, March 28.

Of course, like the Hunkville Centre correspondent of the Hicksville Weekly Bugle, we might state that a "good time was had by one and all," but this would scarcely do

Kalem House—Where Most of the Kalem Players Live.

justice to the Kalem event. The ball started a' rolling at nine o'clock and kept a' going at top speed until the sun peeped over the horizon, Sunday morning.

The affair was really one of the social events of the season. The Kalem players are very popular with Jacksonville society and this was demonstrated by the fact that every person who had received an invitation was on hand at some time or other during the evening.

The new edifice adjoins the open-air studios that have

been used by Kalem during the last few years and is located on Talleyrand Avenue. It is spacious enough to accommodate twelve stages without the slightest crowding and is equipped with every modern device designed to make for comfort and convenience.

But, while the new studio was primarily erected for the purpose of enabling the Kalem directors to turn out pictures in every variety of weather, the merrymakers found it admirably adapted for the tango, hesitation and other efforts Terpsichorean which have swept over the country. The walls that were soon to be the scenes of innumerable mimic dramas and tragedies, smiled down upon a crowd whose mind was occupied with the single thought of having a royal time.

Arbor and Section of Studio.

When we say that the "walls smiled," we mean this to be taken literally. So skilfully had the decorators performed their work that the interior of the studio was a joy to behold. The accompanying photographs give but a slight indication of its real beauty.

Those familiar with the artistic natures of Directors Kenean Buel and Bob Vignola, will recognize their deft touches in the decoration revealed in these photographs. Making use of the vines and other flora growing in the vicinity of the studio, their men transformed the interior of the new building into a veritable fairy bower.

Among the people present who are well known to the motion picture industry, were: Mr. and Mrs. Samuel Long, Frank Montgomery, Director Hotaling, of the Lubin forces; Sidney Olcott, Directors Buel and Vignola, of the Kalem forces, and members of the Edison, Lubin and Kalem

George Kleine, in association with Long and Marion, formed the Kalem Company (the name is a combination of their initials), one of whose studios was located in Jacksonville, Florida. The *Moving Picture World* reported the Jacksonville housewarming.

FROM THE MANGER TO THE CROSS

A reverent motion-picture life story of Jesus of Nazareth, produced at tremendous expense and with painstaking care, in authentic locations in Palestine and Egypt. A film that is destined to be more far-reaching than the Bible in telling the story of the perfect life and supreme sacrifice of the Saviour, in all countries and to all peoples.

Dr. Charles H. Parkhurst, after seeing the film, said: "I yielded myself unreservedly to the influence of the occasion and came away from the representation with the feeling that the transactions in our Lord's life had been brought nearer to me."

PRODUCED IN AUTHENTIC LOCATIONS IN PALESTINE AND EGYPT

The Calling of Peter and Andrew
(Sea of Galilee)

The Wise Men following the star.

"And ye shall find the Babe wrapped in swaddling clothes lying in a manger."

Jesus is found in the temple.

Guarded by the Sphinx

A correspondent writes from Atlanta:

"Old men and women can be seen struggling through a high wind that is dangerous to encounter, to reach the Montgomery Theatre where the picture is being shown. No revival meeting has ever created so much religious enthusiasm and local comment."

The Kalem Company went far afield to make films. *From the Manger to the Cross* was filmed on location in the Holy Land and Egypt.

S. S. Hutchinson, with John R. Freuler, formed the American Film Manufacturing Company, which made a series of Westerns as well as other types of films that featured such important players as Richard Bennett, Gail Kane, and Mary Miles Minter.

With the Universal Exhibitors and Exchangemen at Universal City, Cal.

REMARKABLE SCENE TAKEN AT UNIVERSAL CITY DIRECTLY AFTER PRESIDENT LAEMMLE HAD OPENED THE GATES OF THE CITY AND ADMITTED THE THOUSANDS OF LITHOGRAPHIC SPECTATORS TO THE ONLY MOVING PICTURE CITY IN THE WORLD—SCENE SHOWS THE GIGANTIC STELLA AT LEFT, BEING THE OFFICIAL REVIEW OF THE PRODUCING COMPANIES.

The Universal's policy is to protect the small exhibitor and help to keep him from being crushed by syndicate competition.

"Ivanhoe" Has Startled Europe!

the greatest facilities of any concern in the world for making rich productions. It has the power, the money and the ambition necessary to outdo the attempts of any and all other film manufacturers.

Use Your Brains!

LAEMMLE LUCK

If you are not showing the Universal pro-gram you are overlooking the greatest money-maker in the business!

"Hook Up with the Winner"

These were the men and women who started Hollywood on its fabulous career. David and William Horsley and their crews of the Nestor Film Co., are shown on loca-tion. The Horsleys, with only $2500 cash, leased the Blondeau Tavern and barn at Sunset and Gower to form the first motion picture studio in Hollywood.

The dynamic Carl Laemmle refused to be a pawn of the Patents Company and started the Independent Motion Picture Company, which later became Universal Films.

Mme. Blache and Group of Solax Players.

SOLAX ENLARGING STUDIOS.

Material Addition to Flushing Plant Now in Course of Erection—A Woman's Enterprise.

As an evidence of the renewed activities of the independent film manufacturing companies, comes the announcement that the Solax Company has planned an extensive addition to its plant at Flushing, N. Y. The plan contemplates the building of a larger studio of a permanent character, better suited to the varied product of the Solax Company. It will have a larger capacity and contain many conveniences not provided by the present studio facilities.

The present studio is situated in the middle of the plot of ground owned by the Solax Company on Congress St. There is a small park and lake on one side of the building, with structures representing a small Western hotel, country store and saloon on the other. These have proved of great use in making Western pictures.

Mme. Blache, president and treasurer of the Solax Company, and her husband, Mr. Herbert Blache, have but recently returned from Europe.

Beginning with the release of Sunday, February 11th, and continuing on with the 14th, 21st, 28th and March 4th, the inimitable Billy Quirk will be featured in a series of comedies especially written for him by prominent writers of humorous stories.

Bill Quirk has a national reputation and is a national favorite. Don't miss this series of attractions. They are the best offerings released in months.

"The Woman of Mystery"

New Blaché Feature Deals Artistically with Wierd and Incomprehensible Things and Makes the Spectator Feel Them.

Reviewed by Hanford Chase Judson.

THE newest Blaché feature, a four-reel picture, written and produced by Madame Alice Blaché, gives a strongly-woven yarn of sublunary powers. We human beings live in this, our eupeptic, sunlit world as very material persons. We are awake and we see everything that goes on around us. But let us fall half asleep for a time and things that were not existent before seem to be there now. These things are to us vague, wholly imaginative.

"Dual personality" and "spirit control" combine to make Madame Alice Blaché's latest literary effort, which was also staged for this screen under her personal direction, one of the most interesting photodramas that she has produced in her long and successful career.

Scene from "A Revolutionary Romance" (Solax).

Released
Friday, Jan. 5th, 1912

Our Poor Relations

In his opulence, a son forgets his poor mother in the country. In fact, he tells his wife and wealthy friends that he is an orphan. His suffering mother is brought to his side by fate, and the snobbish son is made to see how wrong has been his way of living and thinking.

Scene from "The Woman of Mystery" (Blaché).

In the Solax production of "Economical Brown" is reflected a peculiar characteristic often discernible in many American husbands. This characteristic is one of extreme extravagance outside of the home and absolute parsimony on the inside. In other words, there are men who never stint themselves when they are "out" with the "jolly bunch" having a good time.

THE TWO SIDES OF ECONOMICAL BROWN

Madame Alice Guy Blaché, shown above *(top left),* who had come to America from Pathé Frères in France, was president and treasurer of the Solax Company, whose studio was first in Flushing, New York, then in Fort Lee, New Jersey. Along with her husband and others, she directed many of the Solax films.

"Enoch Arden."

A Fine Two-Reel Visualization of Tennyson's Beautiful Poem.

Enoch Arden returns to find his wife and children happy with another and himself apparently forgotten. (The surging emotions depicted in the face of the man that peers through the casement at the happy family and finally decides to hide himself away and never tell, is a marvel of facial expression—an apotheosis of the silent drama.)

"He saw another, possessor of all this peace and warmth and happiness....
A child, her's, but not his......
Oh, this is hard to bear.
Almighty God, blessed Savior, who didst uphold me on the lonely isle,
Uphold me a while longer still.
Help, aid me, never, never to tell, never to break in upon her happiness."

Homeward bound, his fancy pictures a faithful wife and loved children still waiting and watching for his return.

She, faithful but hopeless after the years, yields to the entreaties of her former lover that her children need a father's care.

"Philip was the children's all in all;
They called him Father Philip."

D. W. Griffith's *Enoch Arden* from Biograph could not be compressed into one reel, the popular format of the day. This two-reeler was shown on two different days as a serial or continued story.

Miss Rose Coghlan as Rosalind in the Vitagraph Feature, "As You Like It."

The cast of characters includes these well-known Vitagraph players supporting Miss Coghlan:

Rosalind........................Miss Rose Coghlan
Celia.........................Miss Rosemary Theby
Phœbe.........................Miss Rose E. Tapley
Audry.............................Mrs. Kate Price
Duke Frederick................Mr. Harry T. Morey
Banished Duke.................Mr. Tefft Johnson
Orlando......................Mr. Maurice Costello
Jacques.........................Mr. Charles Kent
Touchstone.............Mr. Robert McWade, Sr.
Adam...........................Mr. George Ober
Charles, the Wrestler.............Mr. Randolph
Oliver........................Mr. Robert Gaillord
Le Beau..........................Mr. James Young
Corin.......................Mr. Charles Eldridge
Silvius........................Mr. James Morrison
Amiens...........................Mr. Frank Mason
William.......................Mr. Hugh McGowan

Scene from the Vitagraph Feature Subject, "As You Like It."

Vitagraph's *As You Like It* was another film that could not fit into the one-reel format. It ran for three reels and in the beginning was shown on three successive nights.

The Great Divide, a Lubin Feature, was one of the first feature-length films to be offered independently after the old-line Patents Company lost the celebrated antitrust suit. Shown are the Lubin studios in Philadelphia (*top*) and Los Angeles.

An important early Swiss film production

Edwin Thanhouser, who had operated a stock company in Milwaukee, established an independent film studio in New Rochelle, New York. *King Lear* and *Silas Marner* were two of his feature productions.

A FILM ON WOMEN'S LIBERATION MADE IN 1913

A film on Equal Suffrage

"What 80 Million Women Want"
(1913)
featuring Emeline Pankhurst

Scene from Unique Feature with Mrs. Pankhurst.

"Eighty Million Women Want--?"
Four-Part Suffragist Picture by Unique Film Company.
Reviewed by W. Stephen Bush.

THE UNIQUE FILM COMPANY, a newcomer in the film world, issued a number of invitations to reviewers and other distinguished citizens to attend a private exhibition of "Eighty Million Women Want—?" at the Bryant Motion Picture Theater, November 5th,

The pictures themselves are deserving of unstinted praise. A very clever scenario is always the best kind of an asset in features and the scenario, written, I believe, by a woman, showed traces of talent and no small degree of skill in handling the technique. This feature is not only a most effectual means of propaganda for the cause of Woman Suffrage, but it would, I am sure, be welcomed by any man who wants to give his patrons a high class offering with plenty of pathos and humor. The story of the plot is taken from the life around us and succeeds in portraying political conditions as they exist in this country to-day. There is no more modern and interesting topic than the great change that has come over the political consciences of our people, and this feature gives a most attractive picture of the defeat of the old and the victory of the new idea in politics. I think the love story that has been woven into the film is most charming and engages the interest and the sympathy of the spectator from the first to the last. Those who have looked upon the Votes-for-Woman movement as the last refuge for old maids and cranks are due for a most pleasant and agreeable disillusionment. The heroine of the story, though a stanch enough suffragette, is womanly from top to toe, and both she and the hero look and act their best when they gaze upon the marriage license, which forms the finale of the story.

The acting was far above the average and the director thoroughly understood his business. The scenes at the Suffragette headquarters were infectious in their enthusiasm and just about perfect in their realism. This was of course to be expected with Mrs. Pankhurst to the fore very ably seconded by Mrs. Harriot Stanton Blatch, president of the Women's Political Union. Mrs. Blatch made an able address while we were waiting for the picture and the operator ran a frayed "Western drama" while we were still waiting.

The Unique Company has set itself a high standard in this production and we look forward to many more good features from this source in the future.

MRS. EMMELINE PANKHURST
Great Militant Suffragist, the Leader of the English Forces

This is not a sensational, "window smashing, bomb throwing" picture, but a real political drama, showing the suffrage cause in its true light and as the leaders wish it presented to the public.

MRS. HARRIOT STANTON BLATCH
President of the Women's Political Union, New York City

and her co-workers for the "cause" have all taken an active part in the presentation of their work to gain Political Equality.

We are offering you an absorbing story of love, intrigue and clever detective work, in which the power of a modern Political Boss is challenged by the "Fair Suffragette," and after a hard fight, in which her lover is involved, she succeeds in defeating the political gang. This is the picture with the PUNCH that makes a big hit with an audience.

Emeline Pankhurst and Harriot Stanton Blatch, women's rights activists, joined forces to appear in *What Eighty Million Women Want,* a film on women's suffrage produced in 1913 by Unique Film Company.

THE AGE OF SLAPSTICK

THE SENNETT GIRLS were born when Sennett saw that "a nice-looking Jane" made the front page, but President Wilson was buried on page three.

FOR SERVICES RENDERED, the father of silent comedy, Mack Sennett, was awarded a special Oscar in 1938. With him are two Sennett alumni: Director Frank Capra (*right*), who worked as a Sennett gag man, and W. C. Fields.

VICTOR EDISON'S SELF RAISING AIRCAR

—SKYLARKING Harry Gribbon and Alberta Vaughn

MACK SENNETT, MABEL NORMAND IN "BARNEY OLDFIELD'S RACE FOR A LIFE"

—THE IRON NAG Billy Bevan

ROSCOE "FATTY" ARBUCKLE

SATURDAY AFTERNOON Harry Langdon Comedy

Mack Sennett and the Age of Slapstick!

Griffith's *Birth of a Nation*, to endure for generations as "the first great picture," unsettled the entire industry at the time it was made.

The unidentified photo *(left center)* is of Pola Negri in *Gypsy Blood*, directed by Ernst Lubitsch.

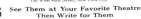

William A. Brady of World Pictures ran this ad offering $5,000 in prizes for stories from which to make films.

The Motion Picture Board of Trade was organized in 1915.

Paramount Pictures dominated the industry in the twenties. Note the misspelling of Sam Goldwyn's name *(top row, second from right).*

Cowboys, Crime, and Canines were film staples from the beginning. *Clockwise from top left:* Hoot Gibson *(second from right)*, William S. Hart *(with gun)*, Buck Jones, a scene from the *Great Train Robbery,* Rin-Tin-Tin, Ben Wilson in *Officer 444,* and Jack Hoxie.

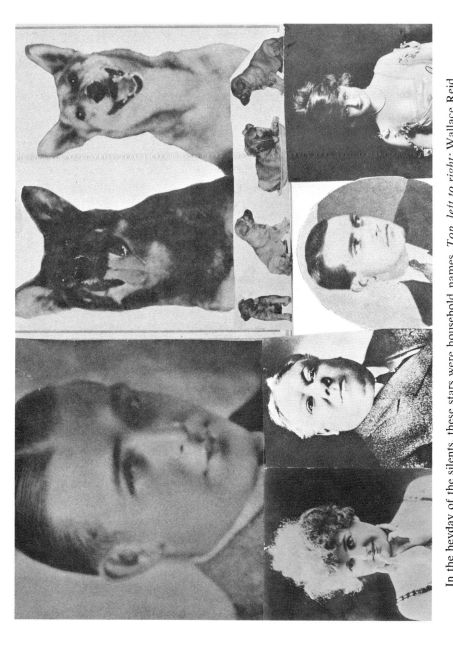

In the heyday of the silents, these stars were household names. *Top, left to right:* Wallace Reid and Rin-Tin-Tin (Warner Brothers' greatest asset) and family. *Bottom, left to right:* Lillian Walker, John Bunny, Richard Barthelmess, and Billie Burke.

No history of motion pictures could omit these screen personalities. *Top, left to right:* Clara Bow, Lillian and Dorothy Gish, and Louise Fazenda. *Bottom, left to right:* Jackie Coogan, Douglas Fairbanks, and Rudolph Valentino.

A composite of films from important early producers. *Walking Back*, De Mille; *Du Barry*, Art-Cinema; *The Hunchback of Notre Dame*, Universal; the unidentified film is *Lorna Doone*, a Maurice Tourneur film, and two Griffith films, *Abraham Lincoln* and *Judith of Bethulia*.

Crandall's Theater, Washington, D. C.

Medjeska Moving Picture Theatre, Milwaukee. One of the Saxe Bros. Properties

New Turner & Dahnken Th Berkeley, Ca.

Liberty Theater, Seattle, Wash.

Bijou Theater, San Francisco, Cal.

Bell Airdome, Austin, Texas.

"ALL THE FIRE LAWS WILL PERMIT"
Interior Piedmont Theatre, Atlanta, Ga. Showing the Crowds, daily to see GLORIA'S ROMANCE Packing this house daily to see GLORIA'S ROMANCE

LOEW'S BROADWAY
TODAY'S FEATURE
A MODERN MEPHISTO
A Photo Play Event

Golden Rule Wagon Shows.

NEW YORK THEATRE
THE GREAT DIAMOND ROBBERY
THE DISHONORED MEDAL
AND OTHER FEATURES

Although rural communities continued to get their movies via horse and wagon (*left center*), nickelodeons were being replaced between 1914 and 1920 by large theaters, many of which were former legitimate houses. The days of the sumptuous palaces built expressly for movies were still to come.

5

Let us return to the days when the feature film turned the industry topsy-turvy. *The Clansman* was repudiated by Mutual, and Aitken was forced out of the company with that film and the studios in which Sennett, Griffith, and Ince worked. Incidentally, *The Clansman*, retitled *The Birth of a Nation*, went on to tremendous financial success. Aitken formed a new company, Triangle, and immediately started to make two feature pictures a week, each one of which was to be "bigger and better" than anything done previously. In an effort to get talent, Triangle bid for Broadway stars, trying to substitute names unknown to movie audiences for movie actors like Wallace Reid, who were household names. Wallace Reid was to go to Lasky and to appear in support of Geraldine Farrar in *Carmen* and *Joan the Woman*. Reid fans helped make these high-blown pictures acceptable.

One of the stars who came to Triangle from the Broadway stage was Douglas Fairbanks, and he was intelligent enough to change at once his entire technique to conform to the new medium, the silent screen. His pictures moved very rapidly due to the athletic ability of Fairbanks, due also to the sharp cutting and editing that was a hallmark of the Griffith staff who made the films. Stories were written and produced by the new team of John Emerson and Anita Loos. Miss Loos created for them a new style of subtitle—witty and breezy, adding laughs to the film.

The Keystone studios were inundated with a flock of old-time Broadway comics and stars. Weber and Fields, Sam Bernard, and Eddie Foy and the Seven Little Foys were quickly overwhelmed by the antics of Fatty Arbuckle, Mabel Normand, Chester Conklin, Ford Sterling, and the other Keystoners. Although I would not go so far as to say that the Broadway stars set Keystone back, they did run up the cost sheets. Far better results were had with two picture people who came from Essanay: Wallace Beery and Gloria Swanson. Another fugitive from Essanay was Ben Turpin, who was henceforth to play for Sennett almost entirely.

Most of the Griffith stars remained with Griffith, although Henry B. Walthall was taken away by Essanay, and Blanche Sweet went to Lasky. New picture arrivals at the Griffith studio were Norma and Constance Talmadge from Vitagraph. Curious and unknown names continued to go up on the billboards advertising Triangle Pictures. Sir Herbert Beerbohm Tree was a sad event in *Macbeth*, although Roy Aitken was to get a substantial return from the release of this film in England. In general, stars of the Broadway stage were a disappointment in movies. A notable exception was Frank Keenan, who mastered the new medium and gave outstanding performances in *The Coward, Lorna Doone,* and many other films. The fault lay in paying premiums to get Broadway talent, both as actors and directors, while allowing the original stars of the screen to escape.

The Mutual system of distribution gave Aitken a fixed and regular weekly income sufficient to pay modest salaries to the many and varied talents on his payroll at the studios. This stopped when he refused to follow the budget in making *The Clansman.* Yet this film (*The Birth of a Nation*) proved that Aitken and Griffith were men of great vision.

The Birth of a Nation opened in New York at admissions of two dollars. Triangle's plan was to make two pictures each week, both of them masterpieces to be shown to the public at two dollars, and the budget was to be enlarged to whatever amount Griffith, Sennett, or Ince felt was needed. Much of this money went for salaries for stage names like Sir Herbert Beerbohm Tree, Billie Burke, and other names far more important to the stage than to the screen. Money was also needed for elaborate productions in which far larger casts, far bigger settings, and far more time was required than anything previously made. Best known of the Griffith films of this type is *Intolerance,* but there were others.

Returns from *The Birth of a Nation* came in from showings in the large cities; no method existed to distribute the film to the small cities. Likewise, the other early Triangle showings were confined to the large cities, and many of them were confined to Triangle-operated theaters in those cities. There were partners in all of these operations. Partners were needed because fresh money was always in demand. Constant reorganizations took place, and Aitken was subordinated to others in the Triangle organization. Almost all of the Triangle pictures were among the best of their day, and some of them were of a standard not reached by the other studios for a number of years. They did eventually reach all the theaters in the country but as reissues. Triangle films, especially the ones made by Douglas Fairbanks, William S. Hart, Norma Talmadge, and a long series of comedies made by Mack Sennett, were in demand for a decade and tremendous sums were made from them. Not, however, by Aitken, but rather by men who acquired them on foreclosure or by contracts entered into when the need for money was acute.

The story of Triangle is essentially the story of many of the early producers. The production of films at a modest cost was replaced overnight by a frantic effort to make masterpieces. Salaries for all people at the studios were to increase several hundredfold. Time in production, and for this reason overhead expense, was to mount in almost the same ratio. The people who were to head the new companies had to be men of great financial ability. It is ironic that their greatest success was to come from the stars, the directors, and the technicians that they lured away from the pioneer studios with their offers of higher salaries. It is ironic, also, that the pioneer studios wasted their last dollars to pay high salaries to performers from the stage who were unknown to the vast movie audiences.

Funds for the production of the new feature films were generated in curious ways. Cash advances were made by laboratories that took possession of the negative of the film upon completion as security for their cash contribution. Interest on the loan was computed on a conventional basis, but an added premium was exacted on each copy of the film, which was sold at a higher price than the market price without a financial loan. Territorial contracts were entered into under which a distributor would secure the distribution rights to a film for an entire state, for several states, or for parts of a state in return for a financial advance to be used in production. Many of the distributors owned theaters and were interested primarily in the acquisition of films for first showings in their own theaters. Under the system as it first existed little control was possible and oftentimes nothing was secured by the studio other than the original advance.

Wall Street financing was to come in the 1920s under Joseph P. Kennedy, but in the early years of the feature film it was not available, and producers of films were in constant difficulties financially. This is not to say that large sums were made on some pictures, but they could quite easily be lost on others.

New feature-film companies were being formed rapidly. World Film, headed at one time by William A. Brady, was formed to produce his plays in film form. Many of the World stars were from the stage, but film names were not overlooked; Clara Kimball Young, from Vitagraph, was their top drawing star. Alco changed its name to Metro and reorganized. In the process, it secured such stage names as Ethel and Lionel Barrymore, but it also grabbed away a number of good film names: Francis X. Bushman from Essanay, Marguerite Snow from Thanhouser, Harold Lockwood and May Allison from American, and Viola Dana from Edison.

The action of the new regime at Mutual was predicated upon the idea that costly feature films like *The Clansman* were wrong and that what was needed was a continuous flow of short one- and two-reelers—films made at a modest cost and shown at a nickel or a dime at theaters that had a daily change of program—the Biograph philosophy of a few years back.

It is so easy to laugh at this. What possible thing can be said in defense of men who thought that the short, inexpensive movies of the early store show days were better than *The Birth of a Nation*? It is probably best not to try too hard to justify Freuler. I am doing so only to this extent: There were values in the early days of the cinema that were lost and that have never been regained. It is certainly true that the making of one great film is much more desirable than the making of short, simple films. Yet the feature craze was to lead to deadly things like *My Cousin*, with Enrico Caruso, which were to prove that feature-length pictures could bore horribly. A bad short film would be off the screen quickly and the picture that followed just possibly might be good. Not so with many a static film of a stage play with little action or movement and with nothing to replace the missing dialogue except subtitles.

The old-line Patents Company, General Film, was to suffer from the adverse verdict in the antitrust case and to see some of its studios leave it. Biograph was to suspend new production, and its releases were to be reprints of the early Griffith and Sennett films. Edison was to suspend production of short films and to make feature films for release by George Kleine independently of General Film. Greatest of these was *Vanity Fair*, with Mrs. Minnie Maddern Fiske from the stage but surrounded by an entire company of capable film players from the Edison stock. Vitagraph, Lubin, Selig, and Essanay were to continue to make short one- and two-reelers for General, but they were to offer their best feature-length pictures independently. Among the films from this source were *The Great Divide*, *Shenandoah*, and *Dollars and the Woman* from Lubin. *The Rosary*, *The Circular Staircase*, *The Crisis*, and *The Ne'er-Do-Well*, adapted from a Rex Beach story, were to come from Selig. *Graustark*, *The White Sister*, and *The Slim Princess* were to come from Essanay. Vitagraph was to deliver *The Battle Cry of Peace* in 1916, which I consider to be the most important film of the era because of its impact on history. The thesis of the story was that America would be at the mercy of Germany if that country were to conquer the Allies in Europe and be left at the end of the war in a position to attack the United States. All records were broken at the time *The Battle Cry of Peace* was released, and every theater that showed the film had long lines of waiting customers shortly after the morning openings and well into the night. The picture drew the enthusiastic endorsement of former President Theodore Roosevelt, and he had many followers who were in favor of outright military help to the Allies or, at the very minimum, "preparedness," which meant to arm and to be ready to attack Germany if and when it was necessary. Henry Ford charged that *The Battle Cry of Peace* had been financed by "the munitions makers," in general, and by "the du Ponts," in particular. So far as I know, neither charge was ever proved. The film needed no outside financial help; it was a tremendous financial success.

Other films from the war years included, after we had entered the conflict, *The Kaiser, the Beast of Berlin* from Universal; *My Four Years in Germany*, the story by Ambassador Gerard, from Warners; and the Griffith film *Hearts of the World*, which definitely was financed by French and British money and which was filmed in large part on the actual battlefields of France. An almost unknown curiosity of these years is a short series of two-reelers, made by a small studio, under the series name *The Liberty Boys*. The films were all laid at the time of the American Revolution and the Liberty Boys were always saving patriotic colonial girls from the clutches of the wicked British. It is said that German money was used to make these films. The producers were sent to jail and the films were stored under lock and key until the end of the war. They did eventually come to the screens of the few small theaters then looking for two-reelers, but they were not effective, if, by this, one is to mean anti-British.

With the advent of a large supply of feature films, business dropped at Mutual. To avert disaster, Freuler outbid every studio to secure Charlie Chaplin for a series of twelve two-reel feature comedies, and the fact that Chaplin was now exclusively available in new films at Mutual was a big help to this failing company. Although they could not block-book in the old-fashioned manner, they were able to compel the playing of other Mutual releases by all exhibitors who secured the Chaplin comedies. Flushed with the success of this venture, Freuler joined the parade of high bidders and secured such stage names as Nance O'Neil, Marjorie Rambeau, Juliette Day, and Gail Kane. Richard Bennett made his stage success, *Damaged Goods*, for Mutual, and it was another success. Mary Miles Minter was another winner for Mutual, and her pictures were second only to those of Mary Pickford in universal appeal. Moreover, great things were going on at Mutual in the way of serials, and *The Diamond from the Sky* came close to the records set by the best of the early serials, which meant that it had a following among adults and was not simply a feature for the matinee shows, as serials later became. Helen Holmes made several serials and a series of features based upon her exploits as a girl telegrapher for a railroad that was kept from wrecks and other serious trouble only by her efforts. But Mutual was to suffer most seriously from the overproduction characteristic of this era. Three full-length feature pictures were attempted each week. This in addition to twenty-one different reels of short films and at least one serial episode. If less concentration had been placed on volume of releases and more upon quality, Mutual might have endured. In particular, if its past successes had been kept in circulation, it could have survived. In the vaults of Mutual at this date were all of the original Keystone releases, including the ones made by Chaplin, the early films made by William S. Hart, Charles Ray, and the great Thanhouser classics. *The Battle of Gettysburg, The Wrath of the Gods*, and the Griffith films were among the films that Mutual cleared off its shelves in its hypnotic concentration on newness of release as being the only mark of merit in a film.

These older subjects were to go into many hands and to circulate for years, often with far greater public acceptance than was ever accorded to most of the new Mutual films.

Alone of all the early companies, only Universal survived through the feature era into the talkie era, and with corporate changes it continues to survive and to produce, with its studios at Universal City intact and in operation both for theatrical production and for television.

Universal was originally a distribution organization owned by the studios that produced for it. Carl Laemmle, its head, at first produced only I.M.P. (Independent Motion Picture Company) films. He later produced Victor films. This came into being when the Patents Company refused to supply films to his Laemmle Film Service exchanges; we previously told of the first film, *Hiawatha*. The films that followed *Hiawatha* were many and varied. I mean, the I.M.P., or Laemmle films. Laemmle was closely allied with Robert Cochrane, a man of great ability in the advertising field, and the I.M.P. films benefited from this. One of the first adventures was the signing of Florence Lawrence, followed by newspaper stories of her disappearance. After the proper length of time, Miss Lawrence was found at work at the I.M.P. studios. A little later, Mary Pickford came to I.M.P. with her husband Owen Moore, and again the industry was told about it. Laemmle was the author of many advertisements that pictured "General Fillum" as a pompous ass interested in grabbing the two-dollar fee from exhibitors stupid enough to believe that they needed to stand for this outrage. From time to time, advertisements were issued under the Carl Laemmle name in which he spoke to the exhibitors "straight from the shoulder" on the problems of the industry. There came a time when the salaries of stars had risen to astronomical heights as a result of raids on competitors' studios, raids of the type that Laemmle originated when he took Miss Lawrence and Miss Pickford from Biograph. Laemmle then said that Shakespeare was right—"the play's the thing"—and that many stars "packed nothing except wads of money in their pants" taken from exhibitors to pay their high and unnecessary salaries. Laemmle believed that one feature picture each week was enough for a well-run theater, and he was able to supply it. He was also ready to supply the short-film programs for the other six nights. Everything could come to the theater from Universal, and the price was right. So said the "straight-from-the-shoulder" advertisements. Many small exhibitors believed him and "cuddled up to Universal and to Uncle Carl Laemmle," as he told them to do.

Many are the stories told of Universal in these days. The statement, "A tree is a tree, a rock is a rock, go and shoot it in Griffith Park," is at least apocryphal, if not literally true. Universal would not waste money on runaway production or anything else. The statement, "Our comedies are not to be laughed at," was seriously made at a sales convention when the salesmen were told that every Universal film must be sold. Still another story of a sales convention of this era is that of a new arrival, a Laemmle relative recently arrived from Germany, who told the assembly of salesmen seriously, "We want wolume." It was to hear this deathless announcement that they had been brought in from their work on the road.

One by one, the original studios that made films for Universal came under the personal control of Laemmle. Edwin V. Porter had left Edison to form Rex Films. He left Rex after a short series of fine films to go with Zukor at Famous Players where he made *The Eternal City*, the final effort of the career that started with *The Great Train Robbery*.

Battles with Kessell and Bauman and Pat Powers have previously been mentioned. The net effect of all of the various transactions, battles, and deals was to leave Carl Laemmle in control of Universal, both as relates to the studios and the exchange system. With tremendous energy, an unalloyed willingness to work long hours, and a personal magnetism that attracted people to him, Laemmle was able to manage his far-flung enterprises. He could go from the studios in New Jersey and California to the exchange centers, and at every level he attracted to Universal bright and creative minds to whom he delegated authority, yet with a degree of control that meant that breach of loyalty would be followed with swift elimination. The policy of Universal was to pay the highest salaries going to the men in its exchanges who sold Universal films. The managers were all competent and well paid. They had the authority to hire away from a competitor any salesman who had the ability to sell. This one asset—salesmanship—held Universal together, and every film that the studios sent in was sold and resold continuously. Laemmle early entered the foreign field and established branches not only in Europe but in South America and the Philippines. At later periods of financial problems, these far-flung branches were to contribute the funds that enabled Universal and Laemmle to survive whatever calamity might befall. As the feature era advanced into the 1920s, the Universal foreign branches were to take on the distribution of films made by other studios and at terms that insured a profit to Universal.

Also, as the feature era advanced, Laemmle stated publicly in his advertisements that a program of short films was survival for the theaters. Well, maybe. Laemmle also had a company named Bluebird that was not a part of Universal; it was from Bluebird that came features to be sold by special salesmen at high prices and in the same market as were the Triangles, the Paramounts, and the other top features of the day.

Laemmle would also divert an especially attractive film that may have been made by one of his companies as a regular Universal release. This film would go out as a "state right special," meaning that it would play only in the biggest theaters of the country at the theatrical scale of advanced admission prices and with the larger share of the receipts going to Laemmle. We have already told of *Traffic in Souls* and *Where Are My Children?* These were followed by *Damon and Pythias*; *The Dumb Girl of Portici*, with Pavlova; *Neptune's Daughter*, with Annette Kellerman; and the Paul V. Rainey African hunting films. All of them were handled in the tradition of the best feature film distributors of their day.

Universal was to be robbed of talent relentlessly, even as Laemmle had robbed Biograph. The most important loss was Irving Thalberg, who left for Metro-Goldwyn-Mayer and who took with him many stars and directors who owed their entire existence in the cinema to Laemmle. Names like Rex Ingram, who was to make *The Four Horsemen of the Apocalypse* for Metro, started at Universal in the one- and two-reelers. Robert Z. Leonard and his star, Mae Murray, went from Universal to MGM and to make there a series of very successful films. Another defector was von Stroheim who made for Universal a successful film called *Blind Husbands*. He followed it with *Foolish Wives*, a film on which several fortunes were spent before completion. Von Stroheim filmed several hundred reels, and the production, as completed by the genius, ran for something like twenty hours. Technicians worked for weeks to reduce the movie to showable dimensions and create a film that could go into release. Von Stroheim was bitter about the cutting, and Metro was able to steal him away, as they had Thalberg, but with results that were sad in the extreme. Von Stroheim's picture *Greed*, made at MGM, was equally long and overblown. His final picture of this era was *Queen Kelly*, made for Joseph P. Kennedy. Mr. Kennedy was wise enough to write it off as a complete loss after it reached the fabulous length and detail that von Stroheim felt it merited. The great talent that was von Stroheim's came into its own again, but as an actor not a director, under Jean Renoir in *Grand Illusion*. What clashes of temperament occurred are not a matter of record, but the film stands as one of the great ones, and von Stroheim is magnificent in it.

Overproduction of films brought an end to many early studios during the years of World War I and directly thereafter. Of the old-line patent companies, only Vitagraph was to survive into the 1920s. Mutual was to pass successively from Freuler to a film export concern called Robertson-Cole, to Pat Powers, and, shortly thereafter, to Joseph P. Kennedy, who was to use it in his many merger and stock-exchange schemes. It survived as RKO Pictures until recent times, but without a vestige of connection with Freuler or the Aitkens or any of the men who formed it. Triangle was to have a short and hectic career with reorganization following upon reorganization and with the complete elimination of the Aitkens from control. Triangle films were the greatest of their era, but cost-control in production was lacking, supervision of exchange operation was bad and inefficient, and too many partners were called in at times when money was needed to carry on production.

Ince, Griffith, and Mack Sennett were secured by Paramount in the early 1920s, together with their stars. Paramount in the 1920s dominated the industry as no film concern has ever done since the earliest days of General Film. Their domination was legal and without any assistance from strong-arm men. It rested entirely upon quality. With Jesse Lasky in general charge of the studios; with producers and directors like Griffith, Ince, and Sennett; with writers and technicians of first rank, no one could approach their quality. Every star name of importance was available only on the Paramount program, except Charlie Chaplin. Star names at Paramount included Mary Pickford, Douglas Fairbanks, William S. Hart, Blanche Sweet, Lillian and Dorothy Gish, Ethel Clayton, Charles Ray, Gloria Swanson, Tom Meighan, Richard Dix, and Bryant Washburn. In support of these star names were leading players from all the pioneer studios, glad to be able to appear in supporting roles. Stories for the films that featured these stars came from the greatest authors of the past and present. Minor Paramounts, like the "Babs" stories, with Marguerite Clark, had been written by Mary Roberts Rinehart. Louis Joseph Vance, Joseph Conrad, James M. Barrie, Maurice Maeterlinck, Harry Leon Wilson, and a host of others were available to Paramount. Tony Gaudio and Billy Bitzer were back of Paramount cameras. Men like Al Lichtman and Sidney Kent were in charge of their distribution forces. While films like *The Covered Wagon, The Ten Commandments, Old Ironsides,* and *Male and Female* may be best remembered from this period, they were supported by a general standard of production that had never before been equalled. It was literally true that "a Paramount picture is the best show in town."

Vast sums were necessary to support this level of production. Higher and higher prices must be exacted from the theaters where these pictures were to play. It soon became policy at Paramount to ask a share of the receipts instead of to accept a flat rental. If expensive pictures were to be made, the receipts must flow from the theater box office to the studios with as few leakages as possible. Leakages had done in the pioneer companies—Mutual and many an early company—and Paramount was determined to survive. Tough selling was the order of the day. Every Paramount picture must be played and at rentals and terms set by Paramount, or none were to be had. There was again an iron hand at work, but this time based on quality, not on strong-arm tactics. The result was somewhat similar.

Zukor acquired interests in theaters upon an exchange of stock, and his theater operations were directed toward the large cities where the control of the leading theaters meant exclusive appearance there of Paramount films, with the confinement of competitors' films to the smaller theaters in the outlying neighborhoods and small towns. Even in these theaters, Paramount pictures got preference, because publicity generated by the showing of the films in the downtown theaters made Paramount pictures the ones that audiences asked to see.

Each week brought news of more theater acquisitions by Paramount. The men who formerly owned the theaters were now partners of Paramount in somewhat the same way that the original exchange owners were associates of General Film. They earned salaries to manage their former theaters; they had shares of stock and perhaps a series of notes, but control of the booking of the theaters was in the hands of Paramount, and the terms were such as to insure the flow of the box office cash into Paramount, leaving little more in the theater than was necessary to meet payroll, overhead expense, and advertising.

Exhibitors who did not like the way the industry was headed combined to form First National to acquire and distribute first-rank pictures, primarily to the theaters that formed and owned it, and secondarily to smaller theaters that were able to acquire a sub-franchise, which obligated them to play all First National pictures, as well as giving them the opportunity to do so. First National's first star acquisition was Chaplin, who had recently finished his last film for Mutual and who did not renew with them. Shortly thereafter, Mary Pickford was lured away from Paramount by the promise of sufficient financial advances so that she could produce her own films as well as star in them. D. W. Griffith, Olga Petrova, Norma and Constance Talmadge, Anita Stewart, and many other top stars and directors were secured. Each such success was at terms that established a new high for the talents involved.

Metro combined with Goldwyn and both studios were brought under the control of Marcus Loew, who operated Loew Theaters. He wished to be independent of his former reliance on Paramount as a source of his feature films, and he felt that the best way to do this was to finance and to underwrite production. The chief asset of the Goldwyn studios was the as yet unfinished *Ben Hur*, on which vast sums had been spent.

Deals of all sorts were made on a new and vastly more complex basis than ever before. Loew insisted upon contracts for the showing of Metro-Goldwyn pictures in Paramount theaters before he would play Paramount pictures in the important New York neighborhood theaters that he controlled. First National insisted upon reciprocity from both Loew and Paramount if its theaters were to be available to show Paramount films. It was a period in which the booking of pictures became as intricate as a chess game. Quality of film was secondary to politics.

There were still many thousands of small independent theaters in the small towns of the country and in the transient areas of the large cities where there was a demand for pictures with action and Western adventure. Universal, Fox, Warner Brothers, now a minor but still important factor, competed for this business. Joseph P. Kennedy's Film Booking Office Company concentrated on this business. So did Fox, Universal, and Warners Brothers, to a degree. In each instance, the strongest selling argument was the Western and adventure pictures, which meant profits to small-town theaters on Saturday night and which were missing from the lineup of releases offered by Paramount, First National, and Metro-Goldwyn.

Fox had Tom Mix, then at the height of his popularity. Mix pictures meant absolute capacity in all small towns, and they were sold at a modest rental fee, because Fox insisted that the exhibitor also buy his other program films. Warner Brothers's greatest asset was the dog star, Rin Tin Tin, and these films, produced by Darryl Zanuck, were the key that opened the door of the exhibitor's office to the Warner salesmen. Universal also had several series of desirable Westerns and a long list of serial films equally desirable for theaters that featured adventure, and although the strong selling force of Universal had been raided again and again by Paramount, First National, and Metro-Goldwyn, Laemmle still was able to secure men of outstanding ability for its sales organization. Joseph P. Kennedy had a long string of Western stars, of which the best known was Fred Thomson. His organization also had attractive pictures for small towns, like *The Third Alarm*, a fire picture, and *The Spirit of the U.S.A.*, which waved the flag well and long. It also had a series of films made from stories by Gene Stratton Porter that were able to bring in capacity crowds.

Universal was able to deliver at least one outstanding film each year by dint of great effort and planning and by going way over budget. Productions like *The Hunchback of Notre Dame*, *The Phantom of the Opera*, and a remake of *Uncle Tom's Cabin* came during the 1920s, and they were good enough and in sufficient demand so that Universal could ask for and get some small consideration from the theater chains. Universal also made a late effort to acquire theaters. Finances, however, did not permit this to reach any important level. Furthermore, the theaters acquired did not always do as well as they might with a steady diet of Universal films. Theater operation meant the acquisition of substantial overhead and this could not be met unless the pictures shown were attractive.

Fox, with the control of important theaters in the New York area, was not lacking in bargaining power. Like Universal, a few important pictures came each year from Fox. An unexpected bonanza came from *Over the Hill to the Poor House*, which drew fantastic crowds in spite of a corny and hackneyed story. A more legitimate success came with *If I Were King* and other films made with William Farnum. *A Connecticut Yankee in King Arthur's Court* was a deserved success. *If Winter Comes, Evangeline,* and *While New York Sleeps* were other Fox successes of these years.

Independent exchanges continued to function with release of pictures made by the smaller studios and with reissue films from the pioneer firms that had been forced from the scene. The Keystone comedies with Chaplin, Arbuckle, and the Kops came back in the hands of distributors, who had acquired them for little money, other than Mutual. Triangle pictures played as reissue films through all these years. It was possible for an independent theater to survive all through the 1920s if its owner was adept at the booking game and would refuse to sign the first contract offered by Paramount. By the use of ingenuity and firmness, it was possible to continue to operate small theaters with a daily change of program, bringing in the variety of film subjects that was so necessary to hold repeat patronage.

As each year went by, more and more money was going to top stars in the form of high-salary contracts. Although the organization of United Artists by Chaplin, Pickford, Fairbanks, and Griffith meant that these stars would take the profits of production in place of salaries, there were new stars who would work for salaries but the amounts must outstrip the salary of the President of the United States or the star would lose face. Each year saw a greater concentration of power in a few hands, but it was not absolute.

The end of an era was drawing near and a new one was dawning. At the end of the 1920s, the talking picture was born with the few spoken lines in *The Jazz Singer*. Very rapidly, all thoughts of silent pictures faded from the minds of the audiences. Every film had to be a talkie.

6

Movies that talked was one of Edison's first ideas, and talking movies were available as early as 1912. They were a combination of a movie film and a phonograph record taken at the same time and projected in synchronization. There were two defects. If the film broke at any point, the voices did not coincide with the picture. Further, the sound was artificial and did not fill the theaters well.

In 1926, Warner Brothers, in association with Western Electric, offered *Don Juan* with a recorded musical score. On the same program several short films with dialogue and singing were offered. These were called Vitaphone short subjects. They did not seriously disturb the status quo. Some theaters contracted for these films and equipped themselves at substantial expense to offer them. Most did not, and attendance was not higher in the theaters that offered sound than in other theaters. No real interest was shown until Al Jolson spoke a few lines in *The Jazz Singer* several years later. Success was such that Warners made a picture with him called *The Singing Fool* and overnight the industry was in a turmoil. No longer would the public line up merely to see a movie—it had to be a talking movie.

Productions under way at the time were hastily rewritten and voice sequences added. Music tracks in the manner of *Don Juan* were added, and pictures were labeled "with sound" to indicate that they had a musical sound track and effects. They lasted only a short time and did not do well. Real money went only to "all talkers." Warner offered *Lights of New York* and *The Terror* and announced that all of its pictures would now be 100 percent talkies. "The Gift of Vitaphone" was extended to First National, which was now controlled by Warners. Fox began to issue Movietone shorts and newsreels in full dialogue, and it announced production of talkies exclusively. One of the first of the Fox films was *The Valiant* with Paul Muni. Although its short length marked it as a featurette instead of a feature, it was the best film available from an artistic standpoint, and showed what sound could do in the hands of an artist like Paul Muni. Another early Fox film was *In Old Arizona* with Warner Baxter, and this was announced as the first talkie to be made outdoors and not in a studio. The Movietone process, which Fox controlled, recorded the sound on film instead of on a phonograph record, as did the Warner process. The former was the process that eventually prevailed. It had the obvious advantage that the sound and the picture would always be in synchronization. The record process was fine at first showing, but on later showings if damage was done to the film, the lack of synchronization would spoil the effect.

All that was necessary in the first-run city theaters equipped to show talkies was to run them off in a mechanical way. No longer were orchestras or organists or stage attractions needed. They could be dismissed, and they were. The victory of canned entertainment over live theater was complete. The fact that strange things happened in the stock market in October of 1929, about this same time, made the change in theater operation all the more complete and drastic.

The first effect was to give capacity business to the downtown theaters that were equipped to show talkies, providing them with their most prosperous years of business. The second effect, much longer in coming, was to take away their domination and to spread business more evenly. Neighborhood theaters could now offer exactly the same show as the downtown theaters. Since it was all on the film, it made no difference whether you saw a movie in a downtown cathedral or in a smaller neighborhood theater or, for that matter, at some small-town theater. Although the end was not predicted at the time and probably not even dreamed of, it is true that the mechanization of the screen meant that the Roxy Theatre in New York, the Paramount Theatre in New York, the Paramount Theatre in Los Angeles, the Fox Theatre in San Francisco, and similar theaters in many cities would close their doors before the era of mechanical entertainment was to end.

It is interesting to consider these theaters. They were built during the 1920s at great expense, some of them embellished with statuary and *objets d'art*. Ornate ceiling paintings, grand staircases, lounge and restrooms the size of bus depots made a patron feel that he must remove his hat upon entrance. The programs given were superlative in a quantitative, mass sense. Stars like Rudy Vallee, who was then at the height of his career, would appear on the stage as part of a stage program that carried with it a musical comedy company of dancers and singers almost equal to what Ziegfeld had in the *Follies*. Large orchestras accompanied the stage entertainment and part of the feature film. Talented organists appeared to play for part of the motion picture program, to render solos, and to lead the audience in a songfest. All of this came in addition to a full-length feature picture, a comedy, a travel or sports reel, a news film, and a cartoon. Admission prices ran from an early-bird price of twenty-five cents for the first morning show to an evening price of fifty or sixty cents. There had never been anything to equal this in all the years of show business, and these theaters were patronized by thousands. It is reported that over sixty thousand people attended Shea's Buffalo Theatre during the week that Rudy Vallee appeared there. The same kind of attendance was experienced in all the large cities with a young master of ceremonies, or M.C., named Dick Powell, drawing capacity business in Pittsburgh; with Paul Ash doing the same thing in Chicago; and with entertainment available from Portland to Miami and from Kansas City to Seattle.

The Depression of the thirties meant that most, if not all, the large newly built theaters of the country ran into financial difficulties. They left the hands of the old-generation showmen who built them. Where they remained with the showmen, the showmen had to listen to the bankers. The bankers said, "Cut cost." To "cut cost" you eliminated the stage shows, the orchestras, the stagehands— everything live about the theater and relied on the mechanical talk box in the booth and the speakers backstage. You had smaller attendance—you probably would have smaller attendance anyway in those Depression days—but you made a profit because operating costs went way down. All the show was on film.

Meanwhile, the small theaters in the neighborhoods were in trouble. So were the theaters in the small towns. Some of them closed, never to open again. Others refinanced and secured enough money to install equipment to play the new talkies. This equipment in 1929 cost over $30,000 for an installation. A few years later it was reduced to less than 10 percent of this amount, and the small theaters began to regain their place in the industry. They were helped in this by the Depression. Some of the downtown houses went to twenty-five cents admission; many of the neighborhood theaters charged only fifteen cents admission.

The silent picture did not die as easy a death as is indicated by a study of what the major studios did when *The Jazz Singer* burst upon the screen. Hundreds of small theaters continued to show silent programs. They continued to do so for many years and stopped only when all of the available silent films were worn out. This was many years after the last silent film was produced.

The Park Theatre in Lackawanna, New York, was located in an area where it was said that every language in the world was spoken except English. Its audience came from the steel mills. They all understood and enjoyed the silent movie, and they could sit side-by-side during such a show. The theater had been well attended for many years. Three successive attempts to convert the Park to talkies were failures; each time the theater had to return to silent movies. With the programs available, all of them from small independent studios, it continued to draw crowds for more than six years after the industry on its major front had become entirely devoted to audio.

The Family Theatre in downtown Rochester, the Novelty and the Happy Hour theaters in downtown Syracuse, and the Park Theatre in Glens Falls, New York, were other theaters whose audiences remained faithful to the silent movie for many years. The Little Theatre in Rochester, on a different level as an art theater, continued to draw an appreciative audience to silent films from abroad.

Chaplin, Lon Chaney, and Greta Garbo tried to remain firm in their refusal to make talkies. Chaney was to make only one talkie before his untimely death. Both Chaney and Garbo were under contract to MGM and obligated to make films. Since the studio insisted upon talkies, they had no choice except to follow orders. Chaplin, in control of his own studio, was able to do as he wished, and he waited many years before he uttered a spoken line in *The Great Dictator* and then only in a short scene. His pictures drew crowds equal to the best of the talkies. Unfortunately, he made few films at this time and took several years on each one. If Chaplin had been willing to produce films in the rapid manner that he did in his days with Keystone and Essanay or even on the monthly basis of his Mutual days, it is possible that the industry would have recognized that the talkie was only one form of the cinema, and that the silent picture remained a separate and most attractive one. I am not saying that the talkie should not have been embraced by the cinema as an advance, I am saying that it need not have been exclusive. Values were lost when fine silent pictures were abandoned so completely. The industry has always gone to extremes. Hit pictures have always been copied and recopied, and the first talkies were hit pictures without question.

It is certainly true that a talkie like *The Valiant*, with Paul Muni, was a far finer form of entertainment for me than the best of the silent films. However it well may be that others would not agree. I mean, others would prefer something other than Muni in this simple, eloquent bit. There was a universality about the silent movie that the talkie was never to have. Everyone, of whatever age or education or interest, could understand Chaplin and the Keystone Kops. When words came instead of movement, the slapstick comedy was finished. Fewer and fewer were made in the talkie era. The only memorable ones are the ones with Laurel and Hardy, and they are remembered primarily because neither Mr. Laurel nor Mr. Hardy talked much but quite quickly went into their old routine of nonsensical action. The best of the Laurel and Hardy talkies are almost as good as the silent ones they made just before talkies; the ones in which there is more talk than action are inferior. Neither Sennett nor Hal Roach was able to make successful talking short comedies, and the old form disappeared.

When we look at a silent movie today, it is most likely that we look at it silently. In its day, the silent movie was really part of a program that included music, music to fit the mood of the film. It was possible to follow the emotions of the players in a silent dramatic film and to be in accord with them. It was equally possible to have a kind of rapport with the players in a talkie if they spoke your language. By that I mean if the talkie was a "good" one, one with which you could feel a contact, it was superior to the silents. I, for example, enjoyed Ruth Chatterton, Elsie Ferguson, and George Arliss, and I was not distressed with people with British accents. I remember Clive Brook favorably. On the other hand, I thought the Western films made as talkies with Buck Jones, Tom Mix, and the other cowboys were simply intolerable. Rin Tin Tin lost his charm. It was one thing to see a fast-action movie with Rinty doing impossible things against a background of natural beauty, all with a musical score that added to the excitement. It was another thing altogether to be told to listen for his bark. Even his bark would have been worthwhile if it had not been necessary at the same time to listen to the conversation of people obviously less intelligent than Rinty and his wife and children. In the Rin Tin Tin films, the dog is the only one intelligent enough to keep people out of trouble. The human members of the cast are morons, pure and very simple. This can be accepted in a silent movie: it simply must gag some people if they have to concentrate on the dialogue.

What I am trying to say is that I could sit in a theater in which a silent movie was going on and accept a Rin Tin Tin movie and enjoy it. Likewise, others in the audience could accept with me another type of story. In the days of the talkie, the common meeting ground was the musical picture of the Al Jolson type, and these were universally successful for a time. Everybody likes a song and dance man, not necessarily only in political office, and the story of the girl who makes good on Broadway singing a beautiful melody with a chorus line a mile long is attractive to all of us. The difficulty is the old show-business problem, "What do you use for an encore?" After a time million-dollar musicals become a little tedious, but nothing else could approach the universality of the silent movie. Some things came close to it. For instance, Shirley Temple was cute and everybody loved her, and Will Rogers was understood by everybody. Yet there has never been in the talkie era a Western star to compare with Tom Mix or William S. Hart. True, there have been adult Westerns where every member of the cast is over twenty-one, including the horses, but the charm is missing. At least for me, and the attendance records show that this is true. More money came in to the theater box offices, but it came from higher admissions, not from larger attendance.

7

The Depression years of the 1930s were good years for the movies; in fact, movies have always done well during a period when cash is short. No form of entertainment can be offered so reasonably. During the Depression years, whole families could attend neighborhood theaters for less than a dollar, and programs of good pictures were available at fifteen cents admission for adults and ten cents for children. Matinees for children on Saturday and Sunday featured serials and Westerns, and often the regular evening show would follow without any intermission, meaning that kids could be provided with entertainment from early in the afternoon until dinner time at night at a most modest cost—the movie house was the neighborhood baby-sitter.

The greatest stars during these years were Shirley Temple and Will Rogers. There was no Western star that had the following of William S. Hart and Tom Mix in the earlier years. Gary Cooper made some popular Western films, but he also made many other types of pictures, and he certainly could not be typecast in any one kind of role. These were the years of Myrna Loy and William Powell in the Thin Man series, of Mickey Rooney and Lewis Stone in the Hardy Family films. Cary Grant, Ginger Rogers, Fred Astaire, Clark Gable, and Spencer Tracy were names to reckon with. There was a long series of musical comedies with Betty Grable, and most of them also featured a name band. Bob Hope and Bing Crosby were popular. Ladies like Bette Davis and Joan Crawford won Academy Awards but their pictures did not do as big a business as many of the others. Records were broken with *Rebecca of Sunnybrook Farm* with Shirley Temple, and *David Harum* with Will Rogers. It was indeed a period when everyone went to the movies.

Perhaps because of this, in many cities one or more theaters opened with an art policy. Films came in from France and elsewhere in Europe, said to be more sophisticated than the Hollywood output. Subtitles in English were inserted in the films because the spoken dialogue was in a foreign language. Ultrasophisticates said that the dialogue was much more frank than the translations. One of the great French films of this era was *Grand Illusion*, directed by Jean Renoir, with Jean Gabin and Erich von Stroheim. The illusion was war—the late war of 1914-1918—and it is possible that this film reflected the mood of the French in 1940, perhaps even helping to create it.

During the years of the Second World War, the movies did very well financially, but they were at the end of their period of greatest acceptance. Certain events took place both within and without the industry that were to bring to an end the motion picture as it had been known up to this point.

There is a constant war between the theater owner and the distributor. Both are essential, the one to the other. The theater cannot survive if a consistent flow of new and attractive films are not available to it. The revenue to the industry all comes from the box office, and the box office is controlled by the theater owner. His aim is to keep as much of the income as possible for himself and to pay as little as possible for his films. Success in the battles between the distributor and the exhibitor changes from battle to battle and the advantage shifts.

As we have seen, the advantage was first almost entirely with the theater owner. The first movies were sold to him at a small price, used over and over again, traded and retraded, and of the sums that came into the box office, only a fraction of one percent ever reached the studios. This led to the bankruptcy or near-bankruptcy of most studios and the formation of the Motion Picture Patents Company.

The Motion Picture Patents Company made the modern motion picture possible, because it forced the theaters to pay sufficient amounts from their box office receipts to make the production of films possible. In turn, the patent companies forced independent companies such as Universal, Mutual, Fox, and Paramount to enter the distribution field; they copied the distribution methods of the trust and improved upon them. The original trust concept was that the theater must take all of the films offered by the trust and make up its entire program from this one source. Although this concept could not and did not last, it was never entirely replaced.

Battles were constant between exhibitor and distributor. Neither side was ever satisfied with a mutually agreeable arrangement, although cries of "fair play" and "ethics" were to echo and reecho over the years.

In a time of overproduction of films, the theater-owner would offer terms so low that the distributor could barely survive. These deals were remembered when the distributor had something to supply that the theater wanted. Warner salesmen were able to extract rentals many times as great as those previously paid during the year, and more when Warner had a monopoly of talkies. As other distributors were able to offer talkies, rental arrangements reached a lower level again.

There have always been two divergent ideas in the industry. The first of these ideas is that the theater should concern itself with getting and holding as many regular customers as possible. The second idea is that the "big" picture should be sold as if there were never to be another one made, meaning that the engagement of the "big" picture must be for a long period of time and that the admission prices must go higher and still higher.

It has always been true that a motion picture company's success or failure is in direct accord with the way its distribution department functions. The companies whose salesmen offered reasonable terms to the exhibitors were the ones that failed. Demands for high rentals were interpreted as proof that their pictures were more desirable and would draw larger houses than others. Offers of pictures at modest terms were considered to be an admission of weakness. The salesman for a distributor must hunger and thirst for the blood of his exhibitor customers. If he does not, he will find that they prefer to do business with another exchange with a tougher policy.

During the war years, attendance at theaters reached new heights, at least for the era of the feature film, and admission prices were constantly raised. Sums taken in by the more successful films reached new heights and, because of this, demands from the studios grew for a larger share of the receipts. This demand took the form of insisting that the most desirable feature films play for much longer periods than theretofore in the theaters. Downtown theaters that formerly had been able to show a new program each week had to keep the same film for many weeks, sometimes for many months. Neighborhood theaters could not make frequent changes but instead must keep the same program for the entire week.

In part, this situation grew from the increasing independence of the important stars. No longer were they employees working for salaries. They produced their own films. They had business agents to negotiate for them with the distributors, and contracts with the theater for the showing of important films had to be approved by the business agents of the stars. There is a sadness about all of this. With sums coming to stars from one successful picture that exceeded a million dollars, it is obvious that a great part of this went to the government in the form of taxes. To express it another way, the system made the star a conduit of money almost directly from the theater box office to the United States Treasury. It is certainly true that the personal comfort and standard of living of all the stars would have been the same—the very highest level possible— even if they had not been as insistent as they were upon extreme terms for their films. It is probably entirely correct that the motivation for demands for more and more money was social standing rather than financial. It was a mark of high caste, of distinction, to have films held for longer and longer runs. It certainly was not necessary. Likewise, it fed a certain ego to appear infrequently, to make but one picture each year instead of several, and to have that one based upon a Broadway play or a best-seller instead of simply upon a good story, as formerly.

Still another factor was to accelerate the trend to longer runs, fewer changes of programs, and concentration on overlong pictures. This was the consent decree, which ended litigation between the government and major producer-distributor-theater defendants. The charges were brought under the Sherman Act, and the allegations were that the acts of the various defendants deprived independent theaters of the right to choose "the best pictures" for their own theaters. There were also allegations that independent theater-owners had been forced to lease or sell their theaters to one or another of the defendants.

It is difficult to assess the exact date when the consent decree became effective. After numerous court appearances in the 1940s, the defendants "consented" to be bound by the judgment of the court in various ways. The judgment of the court was rendered over a period of time. Among other things, it divided Paramount

Pictures (the studios) and Paramount Theatres into two corporations. The theater corporation was known first as "United Paramount Theatres" and today it has evolved into the American Broadcasting Company. In like manner, Loew's, Warner's, Fox, RKO, and others were divided into two or more corporations, which separated the film-producing studios from the theater-owning corporations.

This type of treatment of the distributors had long been sought by the exhibitors. They had long asked for the right to pick and choose one picture at a time and to lease it without regard to any other pictures that the distributor had. Their prayer was granted. The consent decree gave them exactly this.

Under the consent decree, the distributors were required to offer pictures for sublease to the theaters only after the picture had been completed and trade-shown. No longer could advance contracts be negotiated for the entire group of films to be made during the year. As a further part of the decree, it was required that the distributors give up control of their theater subsidiaries and to make them into separate corporations. This was accomplished by a corporate spin-off in the nature and style of the Standard Oil diversification of many years previously under similar antitrust prodding. The effect of this was neither immediately beneficial or immediately harmful, but we will hear again about its ultimate effect.

Now it has always been true that negotiations for first-run showings in important theaters have been on an individual basis with advance showing of the pictures and with individual discussion of terms; there has never been a shortage of manpower to negotiate with the Music Hall in New York and with theaters of this class in the large cities. But the block-booking system was an economic necessity in the smaller towns, in the smaller cities, and in the sub-run theaters in neighborhood locations of the cities. Under the old system, there was a need to secure the volume distribution that Laemmle's German sales manager meant when he told the Universal salesmen that he wanted "wolume." Every theater, no matter how small, was contacted in an effort to get a contract for the year's releases or a substantial part of them. The one thing that a small exhibitor had to bargain with was "wolume." If he was willing to sign for all or substantially all of the films released by a distributor, he could hope for favorable terms. Furthermore, if the contract could be negotiated by one annual sales call, a distributor could afford to make this call. When the requirement came to negotiate for each picture on an individual picture basis, the attention of the sales force first had to go to the large theaters, and in many instances there simply were not enough salesmen available to call on the smaller theaters. Economically, the booking of pictures on an individual basis was simply impossible unless the rentals were substantial.

The power of the established stars and the fact that their pictures were produced by corporations owned by them instead of by the studios, plus the consequent requirement of approval by the stars' business agents of each individual contract were more of the same. In an earlier day, with all pictures produced at a studio or substantially all pictures owned outright by the studio, the actions of the sales force were motivated by the knowledge that contracts for all the pictures were more important than their sale individually. What was important was a steady flow of rental revenue to the studios. Both the power of the stars to approve or disapprove contracts and the rules laid down under the consent decree worked to greatly increase the cost of film rentals. While this could be borne by the large theaters, it was an element in the elimination of many small-town and neighborhood theaters. The ones that did survive charged higher admission prices and, indeed, the imposition of higher rental fees was a demand made by the distributor directly or indirectly when they booked feature films on an individual basis.

The early men of distribution—Kleine of General, Freuler of Mutual, Fox of Fox Film, and Laemmle of Universal—concentrated their efforts on widespread and orderly distribution. They wished to move their films from their first showing to their last rapidly and efficiently, with every picture accorded a place on the program. The large-city theaters were to have a new first-run film every week, while the neighborhood and small-town theaters were to show them later with a new program coming in every day. The concept was sound business practice of the era. It was the thinking of Woolworth with his dime stores, of Ford with his low-priced autos, and of Wrigley with his penny sticks of gum.

These men wished to compel their customers to accept, use, and pay for every release—this was the control they sought. Prices for individual films were to be modest and theaters were to be allowed to make plenty of profits if they "signed for everything." They were to be fought if they did not. Good salesmanship was to mean "get a contract for every film."

The enemies of any form of control say that the demand from on top that "the whole output must be taken" represents an effort to compel theaters to show bad pictures. Actually, the reverse is true. George Kleine in association with Edison was deeply interested in educational filming, and it was his belief that pictures of this sort should be shown. Under the block-booking system, they were. Under a system where the choice of the exhibitor is dominant, they were not. The exhibitor considered any picture that made money a "good" picture and any picture that did not make money a "bad" picture. Yet from the standpoint of holding the interest of the public and continuing to please all tastes, it was wise to have a variety of themes.

In the downtown area of a large city, a week's showing of a film did not preclude frequent attendance at movies, because there were always a number of downtown theaters, each with a different film, and it was possible to go to the movies as frequently as once each day and have a choice of program. In the small towns and suburban areas, this was accomplished by the daily change of program. In both instances, if the patron liked Westerns, he had a chance to see one or more each week, and if his taste ran to comedies or to Gloria Swanson pictures, they were available to him.

The other divergent idea was that each picture must be handled in such a way as to bring in the maximum return for that picture. This led to demands for a change in the policy of operation of the theaters. A downtown theater had to run a desirable picture for two weeks instead of for one, for three weeks instead of for two, and in some instances for months. A neighborhood theater or a small-town theater could not expect to get a new program every day; it must accept and play the desirable picture for two days, three days, a week, or longer. The distributors demanded and got "preferred playing time," which meant that their big attractions must be shown on weekends when crowds were at their best. The theater manager could not determine when best to program his films; the distributor would do it for him, and if he did not follow the dictates of the distributor, he did not get the film that he wanted.

Now, as to the downtown theaters in the large cities, this scheme of things did no real harm. There were many theaters and choice of attraction was still available to the movie fan in these areas. But in the suburban areas and the small towns, this form of coercion was most destructive. The pattern from the earliest days was to have the weekend programs that appealed to the whole family. They featured Westerns, comedies, and, in general, the type of program that had appeal for every age. Pictures with an adult appeal—pictures with stars like Joan Crawford, Bette Davis, Gloria Swanson, Norma Talmadge—were shown at the first of the week when the audiences were different. It certainly is not possible to say that everyone went to the movies every night with this system. Not so, of course. But everyone did go at least once each week and perhaps several times more, because there was something that appealed to him some time during the week.

As the runs lengthened, this diversity of choice, which was the basis for the universal acceptance of the movie, was thrown away. One week, the supreme attraction might be a film with Will Rogers or Shirley Temple, and this had to be shown for seven days. It satisfied almost everybody, except for those people who wanted Bette Davis. Yet with all due respect to Miss Davis, her great role in *Of Human Bondage*, which won her an Academy Award, was not the sort of movie that belonged on a Saturday matinee and night booking. But the distributor said it did, and the theater either had to accept and to play it that way or to go without the picture. If it was shown on Saturday and for the other six days of the week, it was another week gone by without anything for the customer who wanted Westerns or comedies or anything other than *Of Human Bondage.* Thus began the withering away of the mass attendance at the movies.

This was masked by the war. With gas-rationing and other problems, the movies were most desirable during these war years. Moreover, prosperity made it possible to raise admission prices. Receipts continued to climb even though total attendance went down. It was more profitable to sell tickets at a dollar or at a dollar and a half or at two dollars than it was to sell them at fifty cents. What if fewer people came? Movies were still "bigger and better than ever" and plenty of money rolled in.

It is interesting at this point to compare the automotive industry, the tobacco industry, the soft-drink industry and the motion picture industry. In the early years of the twentieth century, the motion picture had the widest acceptance—the greatest number of patrons—of all these industries. With the passing years, each of the other three industries increased its share of the consumer dollar. Automobiles passed from being a rarity in the hands of the wealthy few to being a necessity for everyone. There came to be two- and three-car families and not only among the well-to-do. The tobacco industry worked endlessly to get women and nonsmoking men to accept the idea that a cigarette is desirable for everyone. Soft drinks, notably Coca-Cola, passed from a summertime soda fountain, once-in-a-while thing to a year-round near necessity, to be stocked in every refrigerator and brought home from every supermarket. Alone of these four industries, the motion picture industry managed to cut down its market, restrict its growth, and persuade people to go less and less frequently to the movies.

This process was helped by many factors. The popularity of films with Chaplin, Mary Pickford, Douglas Fairbanks, and the Griffith stars came from their widespread showing under the methods that existed when these people first appeared. The contract that Freuler made with Chaplin was the last one made with a star of the magnitude of Chaplin that compelled that star to make pictures as an employee and on schedule. His twelve Mutual comedies were made within a year and a half (his contract term was to make them within a year), but they were the last that he so made. His next contract gave him the right to participate in the receipts from his comedies, and he had his own representatives approve or disapprove all contracts. Money was not enough for Chaplin. He was no longer an employee, he was boss. His pictures became longer and longer; more and more artistic—and none of them had the spontaneity and life of his early short films.

Chaplin was to join with Mary Pickford, Douglas Fairbanks, and D. W. Griffith in the formation of the United Artists Corporation, and it was this concept that was eventually to dominate the industry. The stars—in the instance of Chaplin, Pickford, and Fairbanks—and the producer—in the instance of Griffith—were to dominate. No longer were there to be a series of films with each of these stars; they were to be made at most infrequent intervals; they were to be shown for many months at high-admission prices; and they were to be handled by their distributor in a manner worthy of respect rather than as something to be enjoyed. Great pictures came from this operation. *The Circus, The Gold Rush, The Great Dictator, Modern Times* came from Chaplin and I do not detract from them or from his great ability as an artist. However, years were to pass between the release of these films. People were to forget Chaplin. With all respect in the world to the artistic value of these later films, they were not seen by a fraction of the audience that loved his earlier short ones. Miss Pickford was at her best in *Pollyanna*, the first of her films for her own studio, but she also made *Suds* and *Rosarita*, which were not ones from the Pickford that was known as America's sweetheart. Fairbanks made a superlative *Robin Hood* and *The Three Musketeers* but he, like Chaplin, took a long time in making each picture and he became less and less known to the public.

The story was the same with almost every star. New, fresh stars kept appearing as long as movies were turned out with frequency. Young people were signed to contracts as employees, worked for a year or two in that capacity, appeared frequently in entertaining pictures, and reached a point at which they could dictate terms. From this point on, they declined in popularity, made fewer and fewer pictures, and eventually retired gracefully, quite often as multimillionaires. One sad story relates to Charles Ray, beloved for his roles as a country bumpkin who makes good. He put his entire fortune into the film *The Courtship of Miles Standish*, only to have it a complete failure and a loss. He was never able to recover his standing as a star and although he did appear in a few more pictures again as a star on a salary, they were not successful.

What has been said as to stars relates also to directors. authors, talent of all sorts. Price tags became higher and higher in all aspects of production. For tax reasons, many stars produced their own films, accepting a nominal salary and keeping the receipts from the picture in the corporation until such a time that they could be taken as capital gains instead of as salary. But all such operations involved the approval of contracts by the star's representative, the booking of the picture on an individual basis, and the demand in every instance for longer and longer showing time.

There is something about the entertainment business that brings out the desire to dominate. The early movie magnates were men who did not lack in ambition, but this ambition was for the fast buck. They started with very little in the way of money, and the acquisition and enjoyment of wealth was enough for them. The ability to dictate what was to be shown in all of the important theaters over the country was added enjoyment. If there was any uniformity in the type of entertainment that they wished the public to see, it was to the effect that the soft life, the slick life, the Hollywood life was the ultimate.

Now with the movies, the domination was indirect and never total. It was secured by the operation of the important first-run theaters in the large cities of the country. Effective advertising of the films shown in these theaters indirectly assured their continued success in the smaller theaters. There was a pressure to show them and to show them only, but it could never be total. There were always some few theaters available for independent releases. Even the large neighborhood theaters had dates available for small Westerns and adventure films on Saturday matinees.

Furthermore, the slickness of the Hollywood touch on films in the 1930s and the 1940s invited the opening of small theaters devoted to art films mostly from Europe. This something different could be *Gates of Hell* or *Rashomon* from Japan; *Open City* or *Bitter Rice* from Italy; or *Manon* from France. Even earlier, there were the French films *Le Million* and *Sous les Toits de Paris* by Rene Clair. There have been fine foreign films from the earliest days. As outlined previously, the Cines films from Italy antedated the feature film in America. During the 1920s great silent films came from Germany, including *Tartuffe the Hypocrite*, with Emil Jannings, *The Cabinet of Dr. Caligari*, and several Ernst Lubitsch films. These great silent films were revived by art theaters from time to time. Jannings, Lubitsch, Pola Negri, and many more actors, directors, and technicians came from Europe to Hollywood and helped make films here that were distinctive.

The role of the independent film is to open up the minds of the audience to something new. Without it, creativity is lost. Pressure for conformity, pressure to follow one success with another made to the same specifications, defeats itself. Any art becomes sterile if it is not constantly to have fresh ideas, and fresh ideas do not come from men who are overfed, overindulged, and basking in past successes.

The little art theaters had a far greater influence on the art of the cinema than was represented by their own small audiences. Creative talents such as Orson Welles were inspired to make films like *Citizen Kane* and *Macbeth*. The former, *Citizen Kane*, reached a respectable mass audience at the time of its release. It may not have attracted the same attention as did the contemporary legs of Miss Betty Grable, but it was by no means overlooked or forgotten.

It has since gone on to repeat showings in small art theaters and will continue to do so as long as there is a cinema. *Macbeth* was not so successful, but it also endures and plays frequently as a revival.

The most interesting result of the art films was the influence that they exerted on commercial films. Many of the Bogart triumphs had touches of genuine art. *The Treasure of Sierra Madre* is by no means lacking in cinematic art. It is my thesis that the existence of the art theaters as showcases for new and different ideas in the cinema was a constant challenge to the better commercial directors. There is a common denominator in the Bogart films. They were directed toward mass acceptance and they achieved it in their day. Yet they have touches that endure. *Key Largo, The African Queen, Casablanca, High Sierra* are films that will play again and again.

No corner of the world was too far to contribute to the screen as long as an audience existed in art theaters. From India came *The River* and in later years *The World of Apu*. From Sergei Eisenstein's *Potemkin*, it was recognized that Russia had a film culture to be considered. The British film was slow in gaining acceptance on world screens. Perhaps the difficulty was in the quota system where by government fiat a percentage of the films shown in Great Britain had to be British made. This did keep the studios open, but far too many of the quota films were cheap copies of Hollywood stories. It was left for Alexander Korda and Alfred Hitchcock to produce films for world screens like *The Private Life of Henry the Eighth* and *The 39 Steps*.

By its very nature, the art theater could never be operated on the basis of mass appeal. Admission charges were high—in many instances as high or higher than those that prevailed at theaters that showed Hollywood releases. Independence did survive in the art theater and it did influence the art of the cinema, but it was not a mass thing.

This was, in general, the state of the Union at the time when television entered the scene. Television is to bear the blame for the death of the neighborhood and the small-town theater. It is to replace all theaters as the mass medium and to relegate the theaters that do remain to the status of art-theater operations that cater to a small exclusive group rather than to everyone. It is my belief that the factors already mentioned contributed to the decline of the motion picture as a mass medium and that television did nothing more than to accelerate a process that was already long under way.

What actually happened when television took over? In the largest cities, there were six or seven television stations. They were to replace several hundred theaters as the source of all amusement for most of the people. In the smaller cities, there were one or two or three television stations to replace from fifty to a hundred theaters.

National control of television was ruled out by the requirement that no one organization could operate more than five stations, each in a different location. This meant that ownership of individual stations could not saturate an area and that total control could not be concentrated in any one person or group of persons. Small, individual stations theoretically were left to produce their own programs.

Individual stations were not prevented from telecasting "network" programs, which originated from sources such as NBC, CBS, ABC, and others. The individual station was able to get "better," meaning "more expensive," programs by making a contract with one of the three major networks. If the individual stations wished to do so, they could produce their own shows and star local talent. In theory, fine, but it did not work that way. If a local Buffalo station had been able to induce Jack Benny to come to Buffalo to produce a program in that station for its audience, it would have been just as attractive to the western New York state audience as the network programs on which Jack Benny did appear. But, of course, this did not happen. (The curious thing is that Jack Benny did play in the Shea Theatres in Buffalo in the vaudeville days, along with Eddie Cantor, Burns and Allen, Edgar Bergen, Bob Hope and all the others.)

Certainly this was not planned. Convenience meant that Jack Benny would do a show in one location and it would go out "network." As a practical thing, it did away with the need to produce local shows in Buffalo or any other city that had access to network shows.

The way was open for complete domination of leisure time, or at least entertainment time, by a very small number of men.

The fact that no box office is connected with television is delightful. It means that whatever is put forth on the tube is yours to enjoy at no cost. It also means that someone other than yourself has the say as to what is shown. This someone is the advertiser. It also might be some organized group that is able to effect pressure either upon the station or the sponsors or both.

I do not suggest that this influence will ever be exerted in a malevolent manner. I do not think, for example, that anyone connected with television would use the medium to advocate an idea that is vicious or repulsive or downright lethal. I think the effect will be much more subtle. I think it will be more in line with the slick Hollywood thinking of the 1930s when the cinema was dominated from the top. The suggestion will be that the easy life, the soft life, the Hollywood life is the ultimate. There will be constant suggestions that the middle of the road is the safest place to be. That to take a stand, to express an idea is to be an extremist. Far better to relax and enjoy the obvious comforts of the good life. The pleasant concept that freedom from body odor is the ideal of a good life fits with the commercials. Far be it for the entertainment offered between commercials to jar this concept.

My own belief is that the most deadly result of television is to make all entertainment a surfeit. Important as I think the theater to be, I also think that it must be limited if it is to be enjoyed. Entertainment was once a sometime thing to be savored because it was rare. To see a great talent like Milton Berle once or twice a year is one thing. To see him every week as part of an orgy of overblown entertainment hour after hour is another thing altogether. There is no real enjoyment in an endless round of situation comedies, spy pictures, crook pictures, trial pictures (all of them are trial pictures). There simply is not talent enough in any one human being to play in top form week after week. There is no one writer and no combination of writers with the ability to feed the television machine with new fresh ideas week after week. This even if the machine was receptive to the new, the fresh, and the different— which it is not. The level of television will always be moral, middle of the road, and sophomoric.

There is most definitely a rapport between an actor on the stage and his audience; there is some loss of this in the cinema but it is not total. To enter the mood of a play or a film it is necessary to physically enter a theater and to share the mood of the characters on the stage or on the screen with them and also with others in the audience. This sharing is something that only the theater can provide. It cannot be had at home in front of a television set.

It is only fair to television to say that certain types of programs lend themselves to the medium better than others. These are the conversation programs, which have the atmosphere of a small group at home. The greatest loss is in the comedy programs where recorded tracks of fake audience laughter are a poor substitute for the opportunity to share in and join with others in honest enjoyment of genuine humor.

First casualty of the television era was the theater in the neighborhood and in the small town. These theaters were dependent upon a steady flow of a variety of film fare. They were already in trouble. As I said earlier, demands of the major studios for long engagements went directly to eliminate variety from their screens. The theaters that did survive were the ones commonly known as "first-run theaters." They were able to continue to get attendance of sorts with the first showings.

Once again the banner of "Bigger and Better" was unfurled. "Movies Are Better Than Ever." While good old films were available for free on the new medium, new and better ones were to go to the theaters. The need of the theaters for something attractive enough to bring people from their free home entertainment to the more and more costly box offices also brought with it a demand for higher and higher film rentals, higher and higher admission prices. To be successful, a film must really be unusual. Ones which were did well. Ones which were simply good old-fashioned entertainment had few takers. All of this was to increase the squeeze on the theater and to divert more and more of the box office revenue to the few film producers who could deliver a surefire hit. Royalties for successful Broadway plays and best-sellers reached new heights. These pictures were produced with a combination of stars and under the best directors. Budgets went into the millions for one picture. More and more it was common to pay a high admission price to go to a theater and to find it in a dilapidated condition. The money that came in at the box office went via the high-earning star, director, and producer into the United States Treasury in the form of taxes. Not enough was left to buy new uniforms for the ushers. Indeed, there were few ushers. Perhaps ushers were not needed for a handful of people often gathered in a movie palace with thousands of vacant and dusty seats stretching to the rear, to the sides, and above them.

For a time the art theater was less affected than the others. More and more theaters were to style themselves art theaters. Yet as they did, the term lost its meaning. The "something different" that the art theater offered could be a *Diabolique*, a *Virgin Spring*, a *Nights of Cabiria*, or a *Magnificent Seven*. Art is often confused with the notion that its highest concern is with details about sex. Some of the art films were nothing more than outright sexers whose art consisted of the willingness of some lady character to take off her clothes and lie down (under a blanket) on a bed with a man also nude, or nearly so. There were even elements of degree in these things. While a certain respect could exist for a *Lady Chatterley's Lover*, none whatever could be given to an *Orgy at Lil's Place*.

Is this to be the end of the cinema as we know it? I say no. While the movie is reduced from its once proud state, it is no lower than it once was when it was used as the chaser on a vaudeville show. Its part in the scheme of things is no smaller than it was in the days when the legitimate stage, the traveling road show, the vaudeville stage, and the family burlesque theater all outranked it. It survived all of these things. If it cannot overcome television entirely, it can at least endure.

If it is to endure, it can only be with small theaters, well run, and with programs made with great care from ideas that are new or, if not new, that have a new treatment. Such films will not necessarily be "bigger and better" in the sense of having great numbers of people marching through Roman streets in costume. It will be the ideas that are marching. Films can be humorous or tragic, mild or shocking, uplifting or downgrading, but they must be appealing. They must be made by individuals who want to see the theater continue as a force, and they must be made for the theater alone. They must be withheld from the television screen. Most of all, there must be a compelling reason why it is preferable to go to a theater and pay an admission fee instead of staying home and looking at television for nothing.

Who will make these movies? Little people. Little people have always made the best movies. All of the Griffith people were little people when they made the Biograph movies. So were all the real stars of the movie industry, from Broncho Billy to Harold Lloyd. These actors will work for relatively small salaries; they will work with directors, writers, technicians of all sorts who also do not expect the big money. Out of this sort of atmosphere can come a *Humoresque*, a *Marty*, perhaps even a new comic like Chaplin or Fields. What will be their reward when new faces become big stars? They can then go on to work in television where freshness and novelty is not so essential. They can repeat and repeat every fresh idea they conceived as young artists until it and they become clichés —all for fabulous returns from the makers of soap and the sellers of beer. But let the little people preserve for those who are to follow the little films that they make for the theaters of this present age. Let these films be kept as a legacy for the exclusive use of the theaters that make them possible by offering a showcase to new talent, new ideas.

It may well be that television will have a beneficial influence on the cinema as a long-term thing. Certainly the men who are interested in vast profits from a mass audience have long since left the field. The studios which produced the films of the past because there were theaters in which to show them, and which could not have produced their films without the theaters, have now turned these great old films over to television; they are currently engaged in making as many more films for television as possible. The technique of "the film manufacturing company" is still with us. It is devoted now to the TV screen and this is to be the mass media of our age. This presents a challenge, an opportunity, to those who do believe that the cinema is an art, and now the field is wide open to them.

One thing is very certain. If the cinema is to survive in theaters of any sort it can only be because there exist artists who want to tell a story that is individual and unique to them. They must be encouraged. Finances must be available but they need not be mammoth. It may be that the consent decree must be reversed. Certainly a consolidation of theater interests is most necessary. There must be a direct alliance between the theaters that show motion pictures and the studios that produce them. Adequate income must flow from the theater box offices to the studios. And the studios, in return, must accept this income, work with it, and be satisfied to confine their efforts to this one field. This is why I say it must be young talent. Fresh young talent cries for an opportunity to express itself. There is no shortage of ability—as was shown when the early movie stars outdrew and overcame the Broadway talent of the early days; as has been shown again and again both in the cinema and on the stage when youth has an opportunity to exercise its creativity.

Perhaps it is time for a new General Film. This time it is the theaters of the country that are in distress. The source of their films now concentrate on television. New sources must be found and these sources must be loyal to the extent of giving all their talent to the field in which they work. The production, distribution, and exhibition of motion pictures is a partnership in which all benefit. There have been times in the past when production was drained of its resources by inadequate rentals from the theaters. From this came the bankruptcies and closings of all the pioneer studios. At the present time, it is the theater that is in the most serious trouble, and it can be strengthened only if once again strong-arm methods are to prevail. Word must be passed from Mount Sinai: "If you want to make movies for us, you must give them to us exclusively and not also to our competitor TV."

The origins of the movie industry were low and humble. Vaudeville, burlesque, and the legitimate stage outrated it in every way. Yet it grew. It can grow again and in much the same way, with fresh new people and fresh new ideas. It may never conquer TV as it conquered the stage, but it can at least give it some much-needed competition. And, in return, TV can stand as an ever-present block to conceit, fatuity, and the like in the new cinematic medium. The hope of the new cinema is youth, freshness—a complete contrast to the clichés and overblown temperament of TV.

Entertainment has certainly gone full cycle in the eighty and more years since the first movie was filmed. Of all of the many hundreds of thousands of motion pictures that have been filmed, only a few thousand remain. The ones from the earliest period represent an opportunity to understand the people of those long-gone days, not only as to their tastes in the theater, but in other things as well. The movie is not the only thing that has been improved nearly to the point of extinction. The stage is also gone in the sense that it flourished at the turn of the century. Vaudeville is gone. Burlesque exists in only a few cities and in a form that is far more vulgar than its predecessor.

✽   ✽   ✽

This book, up to now, was written some time ago. The foregoing last few paragraphs need a change. At the time I was writing, I tried to predict what would happen in the future. With the passage of time that "future" has come and gone. Some of the things I predicted have not come true. I hoped for a return to the movie theater that played to a mass audience with frequent attendance and with "fans" who loved the theater. I spoke of "little people" making "little movies." I could not have been more wrong.

Most people go to the movies once or twice a year to see some well-advertised super hit like *Star Wars* or *Saturday Night Fever*. The advertising budget for any successful modern movie is many times the production cost of the films made in what I think of as the great years of the movie. Indeed, currently it is necessary to spend more money to induce the public to go out to see a new movie than the production cost of the film itself.

The theater as a vehicle of entertainment will survive, but in what form is certainly subject to adjustment and change. The theater was here long before the movie. In fact, the movie was simply another form of theater. For that matter, so is television.

As I said in the first paragraph of this book, "That which seems lasting and eternal is not lasting, and it is replaced." There are some new indications of changes ahead. One of them I have spoken of briefly when I told about *Oh, Brother, My Brother* on Theta Cable TV in Los Angeles. Still another is the work done by the Masquers Club here in Hollywood to continue live theater and to provide an opportunity for new, young talent. I have heard about Victor Jory and his theater in Louisville, Kentucky, and, of course, I know about "off Broadway." Theater will never die; it will exist in some form or in many forms.

It is clear that I have no crystal ball to predict what will happen in the future. The validity of this book lies in the story of the beginning years of the movie, and for this I must thank the many people who made it possible for me to write it. The line about "bushel basket full of nickels" at the Little Hippodrome in Buffalo came from my friend Edward Houghton. The story about the empty office, where it was necessary to call every exhibitor in the area (Albany to Rouses Point) came from Emmett Weakley. Charlie Sesonske was "the wise individual" who donated fifty dollars per week to the favorite charity of the booker at General Film. The town was Gloversville, New York.

Too numerous to mention are the remembrances and stories of George H. Wiley. He deserves an entire book on his own life: producer of *The Woman in Grey*; of a series of Black Diamond comedies for Paramount; of a season of Art Dramas, one each week for a year; a series for Peerless—not to mention selling pianos for gold dust in Reno, doing advance work for Ringling's circus and "gum shoe" work for General Film. It is from Wiley's experiences that many of the stories in this book come. Without further comment, I dedicate the book to him, to Ed Houghton, to Emmett Weakley, to Charlie Sesonske, to the many other people whose names follow:

Roy and Harry Aitken

Max Alexander

John E. Allen

Cliff Arquette

George Batchellor

William Benedict

Wallace Bosco and "Wally"

Nathan "Cy" Braunstein

Charles Dautch

W. H. Dudley

Chester Fennevessy

Edward Finney

John R. Freuler

Sam Fried

George Gilfilian

"Dr." Barney Gilmour

Charles Goodwin

A. W. Hackel

Gus Harris

Emil Jensen

Sam Katzman

Ed Kempner

Morris Kleinerman

Harold Larkin

A. W. Luce

Monroe Manning

Otto Marbach

Frank Mayo

Dewey Michaels

George Moesser

Arthur Morris

Jack Mulhall

Bob Murphy

William M. Pizor

Nathan Saland

Leonard Schwartz

Mack Sennett

Herbert Silverberg

William Smalley

P. Leslie Sniffen

Bill Steiner

Harry Stern

Esther Fetes Timmerman

George Williams

Fred M. Zimmerman

. . . and the man who was my first contact with the movies more than sixty-one years ago—Charles H. Landers.

Index of Names

Index of Films